# COOKING WITH FLOWERS

Flowers: the myths they have inspired and the many tantalizing and eye-catching dishes that can be made from them. From braised peonies to marigold soup, this book opens up a whole new world.

GW00692218

# COOKING WITH FLOWERS

*by*

Greet Buchner

Translated from the Dutch by
Helena Brandt

THORSONS PUBLISHERS LIMITED
Wellingborough, Northamptonshire

Published in Holland as *Bloemen op 't bord*
© De Driehoek, Amsterdam
First published in England 1978

ISBN 0 7225 0422 5

Photoset by Specialised Offset Services Limited, Liverpool
Printed and bound in Great Britain by
Weatherby Woolnough, Wellingborough,
Northamptonshire

# Contents

|  | Page |
|---|---|
| Introduction | 7 |
| General Ways of Preparing Flowers | 11 |
| Flowers to Avoid | 17 |
| Borage | 20 |
| Carnations and Pinks | 24 |
| Cherry | 27 |
| Chrysanthemums | 31 |
| Clover | 35 |
| Coltsfoot | 40 |
| Daisies | 43 |
| Dandelions | 47 |
| Elder | 53 |
| Hollyhocks | 60 |
| Lavender | 64 |
| Lilies | 69 |
| Marigolds | 72 |
| Nasturtiums | 78 |
| Peonies | 82 |
| Primroses | 86 |
| Roses | 92 |
| Sunflowers | 103 |
| Tansy | 106 |
| Tulips | 110 |
| Violets | 113 |
| Woodruff | 125 |

# Introduction

Flowers, in their short-lived brilliance of colour and scent, form as it were the handwriting of Nature. Man would have been untrue to his inquisitive nature if he had not tried to decipher this handwriting. Throughout the ages, flowers have fascinated, confused, or delighted him, and down the centuries he has woven innumerable myths and legends around their appearance.

He has made love-potions and witches' brews of flowers; he has gathered them into bouquets to ban evil spirits or to propitiate good ones. Flowers played, and still do play, an important role on the red-letter days of our lives. Originally flowers grew only in the wild. In order to bring them within easy reach, gardens were established in which to cultivate and admire them, though original strains were often lost in cross-breeding. Greenhouses were built to enable exotic flowers to survive in cold climates. Flowers were admired for their smell, shape and colour. Moreover they were used in food in many different ways, because people believed that such beauty was bound to taste good as well.

The Chinese were the first to boast extensive culinary experiments with flowers. They had many and varied flower recipes as far back as 3,000 B.C.

Their long experience was adopted by the Japanese, who still attach great importance to the flower in the kitchen and on the table.

In our part of the world the Greeks were the first to establish a culinary flower culture and the Romans followed the example in their own wasteful way. The rose, in particular, was held in high regard by Roman cooks, partly because they were convinced that rose petals, used in food, could prevent drunkenness. Fresh rose petals, floating in goblets of wine, were said to be a most effective remedy for the consequences of excessive drinking.

After the fall of the Roman Empire the use of flowers in the kitchen declined. However, in the course of the Middle Ages, the Knights of the Cross brought home flower recipes from their journeys. Increasing contact with the Far East was another reason for the renewed interest in flowers on the table. It was not until the 16th century, though, that flower dishes became truly popular, especially in England, where a whole cult in flower dishes came into existence. The highlight of the cult consisted of a dinner at which the same kind of flower would be used as table decoration and be served in each course of the meal.

In the 17th and 18th centuries the number of recipes in which flowers played a part increased considerably. Experiments were carried out on every plant that grew and flowered and in ignorance even distinctly poisonous flowers such as Lilies-of-the-valley and Hyacinths found their way into the kitchen.

The Anglo-Saxon emigrants took their culinary knowledge, which had been handed down from mother to daughter, with them to the New World and they looked for new possibilities with hitherto unknown flowers.

Strangely enough the interest in flower dishes was lost in the 19th century, only to revive in our present time when nostalgia and "Back-to-Nature" join hands.

It seemed a good idea to collect in one book as many

recipes as possible where flowers are used in an easy and especially tasty way, together with a number of legends, myths and interesting facts about those particular flowers that are not only beautiful, but taste good as well.

## Treat Flowers Gently

Flowers are the most transient, and vulnerable part of the plant and should therefore always be handled with care, both for decorative and culinary purposes. For this reason I give a few rules which should always be observed when gathering and preparing flowers, flower petals and flower buds.

- Never pick flowers or flower buds in gardens or borders where poisonous pesticides are used. Most pesticides currently used in horticulture are not only harmful to insects, but also poisonous to people.
- Never pick flowers of plants you do not know. There are a great many poisonous plants and flowers in and around the home. Keep to the flowers mentioned in this book or ask advice from an expert in this field.
- Do not use flowers from the florist shop for preparing or decorating a dish. These flowers usually come from large nurseries, where pesticides are generously applied.
- Pick the flowers from your garden or the fields, preferably early in the morning when the dew has just dried. They are at their freshest and most fragrant at that time.
- Do not pick a flower which has been damaged by insects, fungi or disease, but confine yourself to absolutely perfect, newly opened flowers.
- Pick flower buds just before opening, unless differently indicated.
- Put the flowers and flower buds gently into a basket, to avoid bruising.
- Once at home check the flowers thoroughly again for insects or diseases, then wash them in luke-warm

water. Strain carefully and spread them on a thick layer of absorbent paper to dry.

- Discard all green parts and stalks of the flowers.
- Discard the white lower parts when using flower petals.
- Use only enamel, glass or pottery dishes when preparing and conserving flowers. Never stir with a metal spoon but always use a wooden one. A good quality plastic may also be used in the preparation of flowers and flower dishes.

# General Ways of Preparing Flowers

It stands to reason that flowers with their abundant varieties of scent, colour and form, with their beauty and loveliness, inspired not only artists, poets and lovers, but also those people who prefer creativity in the kitchen.

It is striking that the culinary flower artists in the East prefer to use freshly picked flowers or flower petals, while those in the West spare no pain or expense to conserve in a culinary way the sweet scent and preferably the warm colour of the flowers too. The English especially are good at conserving blossoms; above all, roses. The American housewives who took the old recipes with them to their new country, however, did not neglect the use of flowers in their kitchens.

They busily experimented with everything their new country offered them in the way of flowers and have thus developed a number of new recipes.

In order to make things a little easier for newcomers in the field of culinary flower experiments we shall devote a whole chapter to general ways of flower preparation. Generally speaking, one can say that all flowers are suitable, provided the flowers come from plants that cannot harm our health, either by nature or as a result of the use of poisonous pesticides. This does not mean that one flower may be more suitable than another when preparing a certain recipe. Practice makes perfect and knowledge will come from experience.

## Flower Water

**500g (18 oz.) freshly-picked scented flower petals, water.**

Wash the freshly picked flower petals and dry them carefully. Fill an enamel pan with a third of the petals and add enough water to just cover them. Cover and allow to simmer gently for approximately forty minutes. Lift the petals from the scented water with a skimmer and add another third of the petals. Cover and allow to simmer again for forty minutes. Remove the petals and add the remaining fresh ones. Simmer again for forty minutes.

Pass through a very fine cloth or filter paper and keep this flower water in very carefully cleaned bottles. Close with a cleaned cork.

Use this flower water only after three days because the scent does not appear to its full advantage before that time.

### Distilled Flower Water

Distilled flower water has a stronger scent than ordinary flower water, but to make it takes greater effort and a dash of technical ingenuity.

Firstly, an enamel tea-kettle is needed for distilling. Place a closely fitting cork into the spout of the kettle, after drilling a hole in the cork, through which a rubber tube of about one metre (just over 3 feet) is fitted. The kettle is placed on the fire; the rubber tube is guided through a panful of iced water before ending up in a clean jamjar.

As a result of the heating of the water and flower petals, steam will escape into the rubber tube, then evaporate because of the cold of the water and finally drip into the jamjar.

The ingredients needed are: **500g (18 oz.) fresh flower petals, water.**

Fill the kettle one third full with flower petals and add enough water to just cover them. Bring the water in the tightly closed kettle to the boil and simmer gently until the petals sink to the bottom of the kettle. Add fresh flower petals and continue until all the petals have boiled for a considerable time. Carefully close the jars into which the distilled water has dripped and only use after three days.

Use approximately half the quantity of distilled water in those recipes where ordinary flower water is mentioned.

Distilled water is more strongly scented than ordinary flower water.

This recipe is especially suitable for the preparation of distilled rose water.

## Flower Butter I

**2 cupsful of fresh flower petals**
**400g (14 oz.) butter**

Wash the flower petals and dry them carefully. Allow the butter to become soft and spreadable at room temperature. Put the petals into a butter dish in a thin layer, cover with a finger-thick layer of butter; add more petals, more butter, etc. Cover the dish well and place in the refrigerator for one week. Use this flower butter with the flower petals.

This recipe is especially suitable for clover flowers.

## Flower Butter II

**250g (9 oz.) butter**
**2 teaspoonsful of flower water**

Allow the butter to become soft at room temperature.

Cream the butter and add the flower water drop by drop, stirring all the time.

Fill a dish or jar with this butter, cover carefully and replace the butter in the refrigerator or a cool cellar, unless it is for immediate use.

### Dried Flower Petals (Potpourri)

Pick the flowers when the dew has only just dried. Cover a number of window frames with net and spread the petals onto them without touching each other. Place these frames in a dry, preferably slightly windy and shady spot. If this proves impossible, spread the petals out in the oven and let them dry slowly in a very cool, open-doored oven. Too much heat, drying in the sun and drying too slowly, will cause most flower petals to lose their colour.

The petals are stored in a tightly closed jar as soon as they are completely dry. This should be done with the utmost care if one wants to use the petals in their original shape, for dried flower petals are very fragile.

### Powder of Flower Petals

Dry the flower petals in the way described above. Pulverise them in a mortar, preferably a stone or wooden one. Pass them through a sieve and store in a tightly closed jar. Keep in a dry place.

### Flower Vinegar

Pick fresh flower petals when the dew has dried. Fill a bottle and pour enough wine-vinegar on the petals to just cover them. Put the bottle in a warm spot in the shade and leave it there for seven to ten days.

Pour through a filter and keep this aromatic vinegar in a cool, dark place.

### Flower Oil

Pick the flower as soon as the dew has gone. Cut up big

petals, use small ones whole (e.g. Lavender, primrose, elder). Fill a jamjar with flowers or flower petals. Pour enough olive oil on them to just cover the petals and place the jar into a pan with hot water. Keep this water near boiling point for thirty minutes.

Take the jar from the water, screw on lid and store for ten days in a warm place. Strain the oil and keep in a cool dark place.

## Flower Honey

**1 cupful of flower petals**
**1 jar of honey (450g/1 lb)**

Pour the honey into a pan and heat until the honey becomes fluid. Add the dry flowers or petals and allow to simmer over very low heat for approximately ten minutes. Remove from the stove, cover with a lid and put the pan with the mixture of honey and flowers in a warm place for 24 hours. Heat again over a low fire and pass the fluid honey through a sieve into a clean jar. Keep this honey in a cool place for several days.

## Flower Sugar

**4 cupsful of fresh flower petals**
**2 cupsful of moist white sugar**

Only use flower or flower petals that are completely dry. Cut up big flowers, use small ones whole.

Mix with the sugar and pulverise everything in a mortar. Nowadays pulverisation can be done with an electric mixer. When the sugar and flowers are mixed well and very fine, the mixture is passed through a sieve, spread onto aluminium foil on a baking sheet and dried for a while in an open-doored, barely warm oven. Only then should the jars be filled with this aromatic mixture and closed tightly.

Flower sugar must always be kept in a dry, dark place.

## Crystalized Flowers

**500g (18 oz.) sugar**
**1 cupful of water**
**1 cupful of flowers**

Use in this recipe small, beautiful flowers, preferably borage, violets, primroses or small pinks. Wash the flowers and dry them carefully. Bring the water and sugar to the boil and keep a kitchen thermometer near hand. As soon as the syrup has reached 115° Centigrade, a dozen flowers are dropped into the syrup. After one minute (no longer) the flowers are taken out of the syrup one by one and placed on foil. This procedure is repeated until all the flowers are coated with sugar-syrup. The aluminium foil with the flowers on is then placed in a luke-warm oven and the flowers are dried. During the drying process the flowers are turned over once.

When completely dry, store the crystalized flowers in air-tight tins, carefully placed in layers with pieces of grease proof paper in between.

# Flowers to Avoid

The fascinating flower recipes of this book may tempt many a cook to try another flower for the pot. There are, after all, so many flowers around the home. Who is to say whether or not many more tasty varieties can be found among them? There is of course no objection against experiments in the kitchen, as long as one keeps to the flowers mentioned in this book. Mankind has experimented with those particular flowers since Nero's cook tried to pacify his master with rose pudding, and since our grandmothers coloured their soups and sauces with calendula flowers.

But great care should be taken when experimenting with any other kinds but the ones mentioned in this book, otherwise the chances are that the cook may not live to talk about his delicious new recipe!

Flowers and plants are definitely not always as innocent and lovely as they look. There are many that are harmful for humans, others are simply poisonous. To further complicate matters there are plants of which part contains poisonous matter, while the rest of the plant is not only edible but even beneficial.

A good example of this is the potato. The whole of the potato plant, including the elegant flower, are poisonous for man. Only the mealy bulbous root is free of this poison and forms our most important staple dish.

Another example is Rhubarb, whose stalks we use successfully as a stewed fruit dish. The green leaves, however, are best left unconsumed since they are quite poisonous.

Some plants are only poisonous in their natural, uncooked state, and become not merely suitable for consumption but positively nutritious when cooked. Examples of this sort are best known among the pod-bearing plants, whose unripe and dried seeds, (peas and beans) we use in many a dish. A few of their flowers on our salad would hardly agree with us, though.

And what of the dandelion, whose flowers and leaves we gladly use in the kitchen? There is no risk, as long as we leave the roots and flower-stalks well alone, for they too contain poison.

It's a different story with the Poppy family. Practically all parts of the plant are harmful to man.

In short, the question of poisonous or non-poisonous plants and flowers is not as easy as it appears to be.

In order to prevent readers from taking too many risks in their culinary experiments there follows a black list of flowers which must be absolutely avoided in the kitchen. All of them are harmful, but those marked in capital letters are highly poisonous.

Flowers that are too small and insignificant to be noticed have been omitted: they won't tempt anyone into making a culinary masterpiece out of them!

When only the family name of the plant is given in Latin, without further qualification, this indicates that all kinds are poisonous.

## THE BLACK LIST

Anemone (*Anemone*)
Anthurium (*Anthurium*) Indoor
    plant

Arum (*Arum*) Indoor plant
Azalea (*Rhododendron*)
Bitter Stonecrop (*Sedum acre*)

Broom *(Cytisus)*
Bryony *(Bryonia)*
Buttercup *(Ranunculus)*
Callicarpa *(Callicarpa)*
Celandine, Greater *(Chelidonium majus)*
Cherry Laurel *(Prunus laurocerasus)*
Cherry, Rum *(Prunus serotina)*
Chestnut, Horse *(Aesculus hippocastanum)*
Christmas Rose *(Helleborus niger)*
Clerodendron *(Clerodendron)* Indoor plant
Clivia *(Clivia)*
Columbine *(Aquilegia)*
Cyclamen *(Cyclamen)* Indoor plant
Daffodil *(Narcissus)*
DEADLY NIGHTSHADE *(Atropa belladonna)*
Delphinium *(Delphinium)*
DIEFFENBACHIA *(Dieffenbachia)* Indoor plant
Dwarf Elder *(Sambucus ebulus)*
FOXGLOVE *(Digitalis)*
Frittillary *(Frittillaria)*
Globe Flower *(Trollius)*
GLORIOSA *(Gloriosa)* Indoor plant
Greater Celandine *(Chelidonium majus)*
Greenweed *(Genista)*
HEMLOCK *(Conium maculatum)*
HENBANE *(Hyoscyamus niger)*
Hepatica *(Hepatica)*
HERB PARIS *(Paris)*
Hogweed *(Heracleum Mantegazzianum)*
Honeywort *(Hoya)* Indoor plant
Horse Chestnut *(Aesculus Hippocastanum)*
Hyacinth *(Hyacinthus)*
Iris *(Iris)*

Kalmia *(Kalmia)*
Laburnum *(Laburnum)*
Laurel, Cherry *(Prunus laurocerasus)*
Leopardsbane *(Doronicum)*
LILY-OF-THE-VALLEY *(Convallaria)*
Lupin *(Lupinus)*
Marsh Marigold *(Caltha palustris)*
Meadow Rue *(Thalictrum)*
MEADOW SAFFRON *(Colchicum)*
MONKSHOOD *(Aconitum)*
MEZEREUM *(Daphne mezereum)*
Nightshade *(Salanum nigrum)*
OLEANDER *(Oleander)*
Pasque Flower *(Pulsatilla)*
Periwinkle *(Vinca)*
Pheasant's Eye *(Adonis)*
Poppy *(Papaver)*
Potato *(Solanum tuberosum)*
Primrose *(Primula obconica)* Indoor plant
Privet, Wild and Garden *(Ligustrum)*
Ragwort *(Senecio)*
Rhododendron *(Rhododendron)*
Rhus *(Rhus typhina)*
Rum Cherry *(Prunus serotina)*
SAFFRON, MEADOW *(Colchicum)*
St Joh's Wort *(Hypericum)*
Snowdrop *(Galanthus)*
Snowflake *(Leucojum)*
Spirea *(Spirea)*
Spurge *(Euphorbia)*
Stonecrop, Bitter *(Sedum acre)*
Swallowwort *(Asclepias)* Indoor plant
Sweet Pea *(Lathyrus)*
Thorn Apple *(Datura)*
TOBACCO *(Nicotiana tabacum)*

# Borage

*Boragie officinalis*

The Latin name for borage is a corruption of *cor ago*, meaning 'I work on the heart'. This 'action on the heart' is a figure of speech, because in former days borage was considered to be a tonic, a kind of tranquillizer.

This plant used to be given in cases of melancholy and depression and even now the use of borage is advised by homoeopaths to people who tend to lose courage too quickly.

In the Middle Ages an expression was used that illustrates the action of borage quite clearly. People said, 'He who has eaten borage can watch his wife, child, brother or friend die before his very eyes and never shed a tear or feel the loss'. No wonder that a plant with such an influence on the human mind was thought to be important enough for Columbus to carry its seeds on his many voyages. When his wandering resulted in the discovery of America, he promptly planted some borage seeds on Isabella Island, and thus assured himself that the herb would help him and his crew fight discouragement and depression. That explains how borage arrived in America from Europe. Today borage is widely used both in the European and American kitchen as a salad-herb, in soups and sauces and even as a vegetable.

To use the rough hairy leaves uncooked, beat them firmly with the blunt side of a knife to make them softer.

The bright blue flowers with their mild scent are mainly used in sweet dishes, but may be added to salads for decoration.

### Cheesecake with Borage

The dough:
**160g (5 oz.) plain flour**
**120g (4½ oz.) butter or margarine**
**80g (3 oz.) castor-sugar**
**salt**
**¼ beaten egg**

The filling:
**3 sour apples**
**1 teaspoonful cinnamon**
**300g (11 oz.) curd cheese**
**70g (2½ oz.) castor-sugar**
**1 teaspoonful grated lemon-peel**
**3 eggs**
**½ cupful fresh borage flowers**

Make a dough by mixing the butter with the flour and knead into a ball with the sugar, egg and salt. Roll the dough until finger-thick, and cover the buttered inside of a cake tin with it. Peel and core the apples and cut them into thin rounds. Place the apple slices on the dough and sprinkle with the cinnamon.

Separate the egg-yolks and whites. Beat the yolks frothy with the sugar and grated lemon. Add the curd cheese.

Beat the egg-whites very stiff, add the borage flowers and carefully fold into the mixture of egg-yolks and curd cheese. Spoon the mixture onto the dough and apple and bake for 50 to 60 minutes in the oven at 160°C.

## Borage Syrup

**3 cupsful fresh borage flowers**
**1 litre (1¾ pt.) of water**
**1,500g (3½ lb) sugar**
**1 lemon**

Leave a cupful of fresh borage flowers to stand overnight in the water. Strain and add a cupful of fresh flowers. Leave to draw again, strain and add fresh flowers once more. Strain and measure the liquid.

Stir in the 150g (5 oz.) of sugar for each decilitre of borage water (100 ml) (4 fl. oz.) and add the juice of the lemon. Bring this mixture to the boil and continue to boil until it becomes a syrup.

Pour the syrup into carefully cleaned jars and cover with cellophane. Store in a dry cool place.

## Crystalized Borage Flowers

**1 cupful borage flowers**
**1 cupful sugar**
**2 egg whites**

Beat the egg-whites till loose. Cover the washed and dried borage flowers one by one in egg-white with a small brush. Cover them gently in sugar. Paint each flower in egg white once more and dust them with sugar again. Carefully place the flowers on a baking sheet and dry them in the sun or a low oven.

Turn them over once, so the bottom dries as well. When the flowers are thoroughly dry and crisp, place them gently in a tin, layered for keeping, and use for decoration on sweets, fruit-salads, and cakes.

## Borage Sugar

**100g (4 oz.) borage flowers**
**300g (11 oz.) sugar**

Wash the flowers and dry carefully. Mix them with the sugar in a mortar or mixer. See to it that the mixture becomes homogenous and let it completely dry in the sun or the oven. Store in tightly closed jars and use this sugar in fruit salads and sweet desserts.

## Cool Party Drink with Borage

**2 lemons**
**6 lumps of sugar**
**1 tablespoonful of balm** ( *Melissa officinalis* )
**½ cupful borage blossoms**
**100g (4 oz.) sugar**
**¾ litre (1½ pt.) water**
**¼ litre (½ pt.) of madeira (may be substituted by port**
**¼ litre (½ pt.) brandy or cognac**
**1 tablespoonful balm leaves**
**1 bottle of champagne**

Rub the washed lemons with the sugar lumps, which will become impregnated with the smell of the lemon skin. Peel the lemons, remove all pith, cut them into thin slices and discard all pips.

Place the sliced lemon, the balm and the borage flowers in a large bowl. Add all the sugar (including the sugar lumps), the water, the madeira and the cognac.

Cover and place in the refrigerator for one hour, with the bottle of champagne.

Mix the champagne with the other ingredients just before serving and serve as a long drink with an ice cube.

# Carnations and Pinks

*Dianthus*

The popularity of the great and lovely Dianthus family becomes self-evident when we look at the thousands of varieties, ranging from the tiny five-petalled alpines growing on poor soil to the frivolous Chabaud carnation from the florists. We owe this abundant variety to the nurserymen who patiently crossbred the different *Dianthus* varieties throughout the centuries.

According to Pliny, the Romans discovered the Carnation during their campaigns in Spain. The Spaniards had and still have a great love for the carnation, which is their symbol for pride and beauty.

They, too, discovered the clove, the dried flower-bud of a tree-like carnation, the *Caryophyllus aromaticus*.

The Clove pink, the *Dianthus carophyllus*, was believed to have magic powers in bygone days. A handful of crystalized flowers was said to give boundless energy and make wanderers inexhaustible.

The carnation is still numbered among the cordials as a result of the experience of the Knights of the Cross in Lewis the Holy's time. They were stricken with pestilence, but were given a healing draught which smelled strongly of pinks. The survivors brought some pinks back to France, their native country.

A pinks-draught, made of three grammes flower petals of the small single petalled varieties in 100 ml (4 fl. oz.) boiling water is still used in France as a febrifuge, i.e. a medicine to control fever.

Ratatafie is another French household remedy for any complaint, and especially for indigestion. For this purpose 250g (9 oz.) of fresh flower petals are mixed with a litre of brandy. After leaving the draught in a tightly closed bottle for ten days the liquid is strained and is drunk from liqueur glasses, sweetened with a little honey or sugar if necessary. The French say that a glass a day keeps the doctor away! It is certainly worth trying, as it is also worth trying if crystalized pinks or carnation jam do make the wanderer inexhaustible, even if wandering and walking seem a skill that is almost lost in our day and age.

## Pancakes with Pinks

**4 eggs**
**1 cupful of breadcrumbs**
**2 tablespoonsful grated mature cheese (preferably Parmesan)**
**1 tablespoonful chopped parsley**
**a pinch of garlic-powder or a few drops of garlic juice**
**1 teaspoonful of salt**
**1 teaspoonful dried pinks** (*see page 14*)
**2 tablespoonsful of pinks-butter II** (*see page 13*)

Lightly beat the eggs, add the grated cheese, breadcrumbs, parsley, powder of pinks petals, garlic powder (or garlic-juice) and salt.

Heat the pinks butter in a frying-pan, form small round pancakes of the egg, breadcrumb and herb-mixture and fry gently over very low heat till the pancakes are light-brown on one side. Carefully turn them with a pancake knife and brown the other side.

Serve hot with fried potatoes or rice.

## Sweet and Sour Pickle of Carnation Petals

Choose big red carnations for this recipe. Remove the petals one by one and discard the lower white parts.

Fill a stone jar or jamjar with the prepared petals. Prepare a mixture of:

**½ litre (1 pt.) of wine-vinegar**
**500g (18 oz.) of sugar**
**5 cloves**
**2 teaspoonsful of cinnamon**

Bring this mixture to the boil, boil for one minute and pour over the carnation petals while still boiling. Close the jar when the mixture has cooled and keep in a cool, dry place.

Use this sweet and sour mixture in spicy sauces or salads.

## Carnation Jam

**250g (9 oz.) of red carnation petals**
**250g (9 oz.) of sugar**
**1 cupful of water**

Remove the red petals of the carnations, discard the white part and crush in a mortar.

Bring the sugar and water to the boil and let it boil till the sugar becomes syrup-like. Add the crushed flower petals and continue till the mixture has the consistency of jam. Stir continuously to prevent burning and finally fill small glass jars with this aromatic jam, which may be used as a glazing on cakes.

# Cherry

*Prunus cerasus*

In an old Flemish town lived a blacksmith called Smithysmith. The good man worked hard, but never got rich. One day he made a pact with the Devil. The latter promised to send him so many rich customers, whose horses needed to be shod that he would become rich in a very short time. But in return for this favour the smith would have to give his soul to the Devil when seven years had elapsed.

Smithysmith listened eagerly to this proposition. Seven years seemed a long time and poverty is a bad adviser. As soon as he had made his pact with the Devil, the King's carriage stopped in front of the blacksmith's shop. The King's servants asked Smithysmith whether he could shoe all the King's horses as they had a long journey ahead of them.

The smith hurriedly complied with the royal request and in no time at all every one of the horses had been shod and they were ready for the journey. In gratitude the King threw him a purse filled with silver coins.

Many wealthy noblemen followed the King's example and brought their horses to him to be shod. They paid him well for his excellent services and before long the smith was one of the richest people in the town.

However, seven years pass quickly when life is good and before Smithysmith realised that his time had come the Devil appeared to claim his soul. Now there happened to be an old cherry tree in front of the smithy, with extraordinary powers. The tree would keep everyone who climbed its branches captive and would only release them after seven years had elapsed. When Smithysmith saw the Devil standing under the old cherry tree, he had an idea. It was cherry time and the old tree in front of the smithy was loaded with beautiful ripe red cherries, because no-one dared to climb the tree to pick them.

'Oh, well, Mr. Devil', said Smithysmith, 'Just give me a little time to go and wash myself and change my clothes so that I will be clean when I join you on our journey to Hell. In the meantime you might like to quench your thirst with some of the delicious cherries that grow on this tree'.

The Devil did not know of the magic powers of the tree and quite fancied the idea of a handful of ripe cherries. He climbed the tree and was immediately captured by its branches.

He wailed, cried and cursed but it was to no avail. The tree would not let him go. Meanwhile Smithysmith fetched some of his friends and they gave the Devil such a fearful beating that he promised the smith not to return for another seven years.

This old Flemish legend may be connected with the powers of banishing witches, allocated to newly blossoming cherry branches.

Cherry blossom is also used to predict the future. For this purpose young girls in Sicily pick a few nice unblemished branches of the cherry tree on St. Andrew's Day, 29 November, and put them away in a jug of water.

On Christmas Day they count the fresh-blown blossoms, which will tell them on which day of which year they will be married.

The leaves of another *prunus*, the *prunus domestica*, or the plum tree, are used even today as a febrifuge and a laxative.

30g of young fresh leaves must be left to draw in ½ litre (1 pt.) of water, to obtain this draught. Three cups a day of this herbal medicine has proved to be an effective remedy against fever and constipation. The buds and blossoms of the cherry and the plum tree may be used in pickles or crystalized to decorate cakes.

## Cherry Bud pickles

**1 cupful cherrybuds**
**1 cufpul sugar**
**1 cupful vinegar**

Cut the cherry or prune blossoms off carefully, just before they would have opened out. Clean them carefully, wash them and leave them to dry on absorbent paper.

Fill a glass jar with the buds. Boil the vinegar and the sugar until it becomes a syrup.

Let the syrup cool before pouring it over the prunus buds. Carefully seal the jar with cellophane paper or molten wax. Store in a dry, cool place for a few weeks before use.

## Potato Salad with Cherry Pickles

**½ kilo (1 lb) boiled potatoes**
**4 tablespoonsful oil**
**3 tablespoonsful lemon-juice**
**½ onion**
**2 tablespoonsful green olives**
**1 tablespoonful parsley**
**½ cupful cherry pickles**
**salt and pepper**

Slice the boiled potatoes. Make a dressing with the oil,

the lemon juice, the salt and pepper and the very finely chopped onion. Carefully mix the dressing with the sliced potatoes and leave for at least one hour for the various tastes to blend.

Add the de-stoned, sliced olives, the chopped parsley and the cherry pickles and mix the salad well. Serve as cold as possible as an *hors d'oevre*, garnished with a few lettuce leaves.

## Crystalized Cherry Flowers

**500g (18 oz.) sugar**
**1 cupful water**
**1 cupful cherry blossoms**

Pick the blossoms of the cherry or the plum tree when they have just opened. Clean them carefully, wash them and leave them to dry on absorbent kitchen paper. Boil the water and the sugar but keep an eye on the temperature. As soon as it has reached about 115°C, drop a few flowers into the syrup. Do not leave them for more than half a minute. Take them out carefully and place them on a piece of aluminium foil to dry. Continue until all flowers have been immersed in the sugar syrup.

The blossoms can be dried in the sunshine, but if there is no sun, they may equally well be placed in a very moderate oven on a baking sheet covered with aluminium foil. The oven door should be kept open and each flower will have to be turned once during the drying process.

When the blossoms are thoroughly dry, they are placed very gently in an airtight tin or container. Store them in a cool dry place.

# Chrysanthemums

*Chrysanthemum indicum*

The chrysanthemum plays no part in our Western folklore. It does not grow in our countries as a wild flower, though we do have some indigenous chrysanthemum varieties. We count the wild marigold and daisy family among them, e.g. the Ox-eye daisy (*Chrysanthemum leucanthemum*). Some people even include tansy under the name of *Chrysanthemum vulgare*. The *Chrysanthemum indicum*, of which roughly 30,000 varieties are known, is a newcomer in our part of the world. For legends about the chrysanthemum we shall have to go to the Far East, China and Japan. They can proudly claim the experience of at least two thousand years of growing and preparing chrysanthemums.

Chrysanthemums are very popular in China and Japan, and are symbolic of a quiet, withdrawn life. Especially in China the consumption of chrysanthemums is believed to prevent and even cure the infirmities of old age. Some stories want us to believe that chrysanthemum flowers make the body supple, the hair black, and worn out teeth strong again. Those of us who would rather not start a chrysanthemum-laden diet, could make do with pills prepared from the stalks and roots of certain chrysanthemum varieties. The Japanese, like the

Chinese, are very fond of this flower: it is the personal emblem of their Emperor. And, according to some well-informed people, the red circle on the Japanese flag does not represent the sun, but a chrysanthemum with sixteen petals fitting closely and perfectly round a flowerheart.

The following recipes are mainly of Japanese origin, because today the chrysanthemum plays a more important role in the Japanese kitchen than in the Chinese.

### Chrysanthemum Soup

1 litre (1¾ pt.) milk
3 tablespoonsful cornflour
salt
pepper
2 large yellow chrysanthemums and several small
    yellow chrysanthemums

Bring the milk to the boil. Dissolve the cornflour in a few spoonfuls of cold milk and use to bind the boiling milk. Keep warm.

Carefully pick the petals of the chrysanthemums, chop small and bring to the boil in very little water. Take off the stove as soon as they boil and stir the chopped petals into the soup. Season with the pepper and salt and serve as hot as possible.

### Chrysanthemum Salad I

500g (18 oz.) boiled potatoes
20 small chrysanthemums
1 tablespoonful capers
4 tablespoonsful oil
3 tablespoonsful vinegar
¼ onion
salt          mustard
pepper        sugar

Make a salad dressing of the oil, vinegar, finely chopped onion, salt, pepper, a little French mustard, and a pinch of sugar. Slice the potatoes, preferably while still warm, into the dressing and mix well. Add the capers and finally the petals of the chrysanthemums.

These are first gently picked from the flowers, washed, carefully dried and finally blanched for a short while in boiling water with some salt and a drop of vinegar. Drain the petals and mix into the salad shortly before serving.

## Chrysanthemum Salad II

1 cupful white chrysanthemum petals
1 cupful yellow chrysanthemum petals
2 cupsful green pansy or violet leaves
finely chopped lettuce (optional)
2 tablespoonsful oil
1 tablespoonful vinegar
1 teaspoonful sugar
salt
pepper
1 cupful rose-petals

Wash the flower petals and dry them carefully. Discard the lower white parts of the rose-petals. Mix the petals with the violet leaves or lettuce. Put into a salad bowl and chill thoroughly.

Make a dressing of the oil, vinegar, sugar, salt and pepper and add this to the salad shortly before serving.

## Tea with Conserved Chrysanthemum Flowers

2 cupsful of small chrysanthemum flowers
2 cupsful water
$\frac{1}{2}$ cupful salt
2 small sour plums (dark purple)

Fill a glass jar or earthenware pot with fresh, washed and dried chrysanthemum flowers.

Dissolve the salt in the water, heat the water if necessary, but allow it to cool afterwards. Place the two plums on top of the chrysanthemums and fill the jar with the brine. Place a clean cheese cloth over the jar and tighten this by placing a stone in the jar opening.

Store in a dry cool place. Check occasionally for mildew. Leave to draw for seven months. Remove the flowers one by one from the pot, rinse to remove the salt and use to make tea combined with ordinary tea.

Serve this spicy refreshing tea on hot summer days, for this drink has an extraordinary cooling effect.

## Chrysanthemum Croquettes with Lentils

**250g (9 oz.) lentils**
**½ cupful finely chopped chrysanthemum petals**
**salt**
**pepper**
**paprika**
**1 egg**
**breadcrumbs**
**oil to fry**

Soak the lentils overnight and bring to the boil in the soaking water. When done, pass through a sieve or use mixer to *purée* them.

Mix the stiff lentil *purée* with the finely chopped onions, the washed, dried and chopped chrysanthemum petals, salt, pepper and a pinch of paprika.

Make approximately twelve croquettes (round, flat shapes) from the mixture. Coat these with beaten egg, then with breadcrumbs, and fry these croquettes in hot oil until nicely brown. Serve hot with rice or potatoes.

# Clover

*Trifolium pratense*

For some mysterious reason a number of the ordinary trefoil-leaved clover grow into a four-leaved variety. The rarity of this phenomenom has always stimulated people's imagination and in almost every Western country the four-leaved clover is considered lucky. These leaves should be treated with care, though, because things will not look so good for the unlucky man or woman who treads bare-foot on a four-leaved clover. The luck-bringing power will instantly change into an evil force, causing fever.

Legend has it that four-leaved clover was used in Flanders in early centuries in treasure-hunting. In France it helped to convict witches. The four-leaved clover was placed in the holy water font near the exit of the church and the witch who sprinkled herself with this holy water could immediately be recognised by a red reflection of fire around her head.

For safety's sake the witch-hunters claimed that this reflection was only visible to priests and 'initiates', whoever they may have been.

In Friesland not only four-leaved clover but clover in general played an important part in the life of the magician Klaas Kunst, also known as Klaas Gerrit Wiersma.

Klaas Kunst was known for his magic gift for miles around. He was not only a wizard: he was also a highly religious man who loyally went to church each Sunday. However, one unfortunate Sunday, Klaas forgot to lock the room where he kept his book of spells. His young apprentice took this opportunity to discover his master's secrets. He started to leaf busily through the book in search of a small simple spell. As soon as he had turned a few pages a swarm of black rooks flew into the room through the open window. The rooks settled all over the room and the more the apprentice tried to read the book the more rooks entered the room, until finally the apprentice took fright and fled from the room.

Meanwhile, Klaas Kunst was in church, and being a real sorcerer knew exactly what was happening at home. In order to prevent further mischief, he decided to leave immediately after the sermon and to go home. Upon arrival, he found not only his helpless and frightened apprentice but also a room black with rooks.

Klaas Kunst tried to dislodge the rooks by reading everything his apprentice had read during his absence once more, but this time back to front. It did not work.

Thereupon Klaas Kunst fetched two sacks of clover-seed from his barn and scattered the seed onto the floor in his room mumbling 'Two men, one seed'. The rooks understood that their presence was no longer necessary, pecked up the seed and flew from the room in pairs never to return again. This illustrates the magical powers of four-leaved clover and clover seed.

The small aromatic flowers do not possess such powers, but they do help against depression and melancholy, provided the flowers are prepared in the right way.

Thos who would like to try it should boil a handful of clover-blossom, a handful of camomile flowers and a handful of mallow flowers in ample water. After a quarter of an hour, this scented mixture must be strained and added to the bath-water. All that remains to be done is to take a bath in this flower water and the world will appear to be a brighter place, that is, if we are to believe the old chronicles.

## Clover Sandwiches

**8 slices of white bread without the crusts**
**1 cupful of clover flowers**
**butter**

Generously butter four slices of bread and divide the washed and dried clover blossom among them. Let the flowers overflow the edge of the sandwich.

Butter the remaining four slices of bread, press them onto the clover covered slices and cut the sandwich diagonally across.

Serve the sandwiches as cold as possible, garnished with fresh clover flowers if wanted.

## Sweet and Sour Pickle of Clover Flowers

**1 litre measure filled with clover flowers**
**$\frac{3}{4}$ litre (1$\frac{1}{2}$ pt.) wine vinegar**
**750g (26 oz.) sugar**

Carefully discard all green parts of the clover flowers, wash and dry them.

Fill a glass or earthenware jar with the flowers. Bring the vinegar and the sugar to the boil, leave to boil until the sugar is completely dissolved and the liquid has a light syrup-like consistency. Let the liquid cool and pour it over the flowers until they are completely covered.

Cover with cellophane and leave in a cool dark place. Store for a few weeks before using this pickle with spicy dishes.

## Clover Wine

**1 litre measure of red clover blossoms**
**2 kilos sugar**
**2 oranges**
**3 lemons**
**20g (¾ oz.) yeast**

Pick the flowers of the clover on a dry sunny day, for they will be at their most aromatic then. Gently discard all green parts of the flowers.

Fill a large earthenware jar with the clover flowers. Bring the water to the boil and pour it boiling over the flowers. As soon as the water has cooled, the sliced citrus-fruit and the sugar are added.

Dissolve the yeast in a little lukewarm water and add it to the other ingredients.

Cover it with a cloth and leave at room temperature for five days, but stir it well with a wooden spoon at least twice a day.

Strain after another five days at room-temperature covered with a cloth.

Strain once more through a very fine cloth and leave covered for three more days.

Fill well-cleaned bottles with the wine, but close them only lightly, for there is still a chance of fermentation.

Cork the bottles when the fermentation has stopped, which is usually ten days to a fortnight after bottling.

Store the bottles of clover wine in a cool dark place for a minimum of four weeks before use.

# Coltsfoot

*Tussilago farfara*

Although coltsfoot was known and praised for its healing powers many centuries ago, its name does not appear in the *Capitulare de Villis*, the volume of rules and regulations issued by Charlemagne for the management of his landed and domanial estates. Presumably coltsfoot was such a well-known and well-established weed that it was not considered necessary to grow it specifically.

Even today we find coltsfoot in the most unexpected places, such as wastelands in the middle of a town, where this lime-loving plant is often the only plant to flourish.

Coltsfoot derives its English name from the likeness of its leaf to a horse's hoof. The Latin name points at the healing power of the plant and is derived from *tussis* meaning cough and *ago* meaning to chase away. Coltsfoot was and still is considered to be one of the best cough medicines.

Even Pliny mentions the customs of burning the roots of coltsfoot on a fire of cedar-wood and inhaling the fumes to ease a cough.

In many regions children are given an extract of 30g dried flowers or leaves in one litre of water to relieve their coughs. After drawing for five minutes the extract must be strained, especially when the flowers are being used, since the pappus might irritate the mucous membranes. Taken regularly with some honey, this draught is among the best and most innocent cough mixtures.

People who want to pick coltsfoot flowers should go about this early in spring, for the bright yellow flowers emerge as early as the end of February, or the beginning of March. The leaves are formed later, hence its mediaeval name, *fillus ante patrem*, meaning the son before the father.

The leaves were and still are, eaten as an early Spring vegetable, prepared like spinach.

The flowers may be floated in a bottle of sherry, three at a time. They not only give a sparkling colour to the sherry, but also enrich it with a very special aroma.

## Pancakes with Coltsfoot Petals

$\frac{1}{2}$ cupful petals of coltsfoot flowers
250g (19 oz.) flour
1 egg
10g ($\frac{1}{2}$ oz.) yeast)
$4\frac{1}{2}$ decilitres (160 fl. oz.) milk (lukewarm)
oil or butter for frying

Pick the flowers when the sun is shining. They will be open. Wash the flowers carefully, dry them well and pull out the yellow petals one by one.

Put the flour into a bowl and make a depression in the middle. Mix half the lukewarm milk and the yeast, pour into the flour and make a smooth mixture, stirring from the middle. Slowly pour the remaining milk into the mixture stirring constantly and finally add the coltsfoot petals.

Leave the dough to prove for one hour in a warm place covered with a cloth. Heat some butter or oil in a frying pan till very hot and pour in some of the pancake mixture. Slowly brown the pancake on one side, then the other side.

Make four or five pancakes in this way and serve hot with syrup or honey.

## Wine of Coltsfoot Flowers

**1 litre jug filled with coltsfoot flowers**
**4 litres water (7 pt.)**
**1,500g (1¼ lb) sugar**
**2 tablespoonsful raisins**
**3 oranges**
**2 lemons**
**20g (¾ oz.) yeast**

Pick the flowers on a sunny day, wash them and allow them to dry on a layer of absorbent paper.

Place the flowers in a large bowl and pour the boiling water over them. Allow this mixture to stand for three days, stirring occasionally, and cover with a cloth to prevent dust falling into it.

Strain the mixture after three days and boil the clear liquid with the sugar for half an hour. The yeast is added when the liquid has cooled and the raisins and sliced oranges and lemons are put in as well.

Leave this mixture to ferment, covered with a cloth, for three months. Bottle the wine when the fermenting has stopped.

Keep this wine for several weeks before drinking.

# Daisies

*Bellis perennis*

When the Archangel Gabriel told Mary that she would become the mother of God's Son, she was moved to tears. The tears ran down her cheeks and some fell to the ground and formed many small dark patches on the trampled mud floor.

God saw her tears and promptly changed them into bright daisies to honour the future mother of His Son. The Devil, however, saw the tears as well, for he was listening behind the curtain, as usual, because he wanted to keep his eye on the comings and goings of Gabriel, his arch-enemy. When he saw each tear of the young woman change into a lovely flower he became furious. Wasn't it bad enough that the Saviour of Man, the fighter of the Devil was to be born? Did even tears have to change into pretty flowers? The Devil could not bear to look at them any longer and enraged, he extended his stinking claws to pull out the flowers as quickly as they had come up, but the flowers created by God appeared to be stronger than the claws of the Devil. They were so firmly rooted and so invulnerable against the Devil's touch, that they happily went on growing and flowering.

However, in each place where the devilish claws had touched the ground another plant sprang up, the strongly scented garlic.

From that moment onwards, daisies and garlic could not tolerate one another. In fields the little daisy will always banish the garlic until it only flowers near the edges, so that the daisy keeps the sole right to the tender green meadows of Spring. Spring and daisies belong together.

Many centuries ago, the daisy played an important part in the lives of the young knights in England. They were allowed to add a daisy to their coat of arms, when their highly-born love had consented to marry them. This is why today many a British coat of arms is decorated with a daisy.

If the young maiden was uncertain of her feelings towards the young knight, daisies played a part as well. She would make a daisy-chain which she would give to the knight as a temporary rejection.

On the Continent too, the daisy is used by young lovers, though differently. There it plays the part of the oracle.

Young girls in love pull out the petals one by one reciting a little poem: 'Noblewoman, beggarwoman, townswoman.' They would discover their future prospects, for the last petal would tell them.

In Switzerland, a similar rhyme exists. The young girls there pull out the petals, saying, 'ledig sin, Hochzeit hab'n, ins Chlösterle gehn' (spinsterhood, marriage, to the nunnery). The daisy is considered to be bringer of good luck as well as an oracle-flower, provided it is picked between midnight and one o'clock in the morning on Midsummer's night, the night of 24 June. These particular daisies have the magic power to keep all misfortune away from whoever picks and wears them. For those who dislike nightly excursions into the fields, it is a comforting thought that the first three daisies found in Spring will protect the finder from tooth-ache and eye infections for a full year provided he or she eats them on the spot! This custom is understandable, for in some parts of Europe, fresh daisy leaves are chewed to help cure mouth infections.

The boiled leaves are used to make rich food more palatable and more digestible, but this book is primarily concerned with the use of flowers, so we shall leave the use of daisy leaves aside.

In the following recipes only the flowers of the daisy are being used: white rays which are at times tipped in a delicate red. The red is said to have come from a drop of blood of Holy Mary when she hurt her finger while adorning her Child's coverlet with daisies.

## Daisy Salad

**2 heads of lettuce**
**1 cupful fresh daisies**
**3 tablespoonsful oil**
**1 tablespoonful wine vinegar**
**parsley**
**chives**
**basil**
**salt**
**pepper**
**sugar**
**1 hard-boiled egg**

Peel and mash the hard-boiled egg with a fork and mix it with the oil, pepper, salt and sugar. When mixed well, add the vinegar and the finely chopped fresh herbs. Discard the rough outer leaves of the lettuces, discard the stalks and tear the leaves carefully into small pieces. Wash and drain the lettuce.

Wash the daisies and drain or leave them to dry on absorbent kitchen paper.

Mix two thirds of the daisy flowers with the lettuce, add the dressing and toss gently.

Garnish the salad with the remainder of the daisies.

## Daisy Wine

**1 litre (1¾ pt.) jug filled with freshly picked daisies**
**4 litres (7 pt.) water**
**15g (1 oz.) fresh yeast**
**2 lemons**
**2 oranges**
**1 cupful raisins**
**1½ kilos (3¼ lb) sugar**

Pour the four litres of boiling water onto the carefully cleaned daisies and leave in a cool place for twenty-four hours. Cover to avoid dust.

Strain the water and boil for ten more minutes. Leave to cool until lukewarm and add the yeast, the sliced (but not peeled) oranges and lemons, the raisins and the sugar. Stir thoroughly and leave the mixture to ferment in a cool place for three weeks. Skim and filter through a fine cloth.

Fill carefully cleaned bottles with this young wine, cork them tightly and store, on their sides, for several weeks before use.

# Dandelions

*Taraxacum officinale*

The Greeks thought that the dandelion owed its existence to the Sun God who daily rushed along the heavens in his golden chariot.

Dandelions sprang up from the dust his chariot threw up and they took the shape and the colour of the Sun God.

But this almost divine origin had nothing to do with the naming of the flower.

The Greeks appreciated the qualities of the dandelion, whose juice is used to cure certain eye-ailments, much more than its close ties to a deity. They therefore derived its name from the word *Taraxis*, i.e. the name of a certain eye infection, and the word *akoemai*, meaning 'to heal'.

In later centuries, the genetic name *officinale* was added and this also indicates its healing powers. Its leaves were and indeed still are used as a medicine for gall and liver disorders. Today the dandelion still plays an important part in the so-called 'Spring cure', intended to free the body of all the results of Winter's rich and heavy foods. However, humankind are not the only ones to recognise the medicinal value of the dandelion. Horses are aware of it, hence the name that is frequently used on the continent, 'Horse flower'.

It is also called 'Rabbit leaf', since rabbits seem to like it even better than the horses do.

The name 'Letter bearer' which is frequently used in various parts of the Netherlands and Belgium is a more charming name for this common flower. This name is connected to the fluffy umbrella-like seeds that gaily sail through the summer air. The fluffy seeds give the dandelion its value as an oracle-flower. In many parts of Europe a young girl blows at the fluffy seeds of the ripened dandelion. The number of times she has to blow before the last seed-umbrella takes to the air determines the number of years she will have to wait for her wedding day.

The young girls in Flanders blow three times and count the left-over seeds. The number tells them how many years of spinsterhood they have before them.

But the dandelion is more than an oracle-flower, fodder or a medicinal herb.

The dandelion can very well be eaten and formed part of the staple diet for many centuries, mainly because dandelions are always abundant everywhere during the summer months.

The fresh leaves were and are used in salads, as a vegetable and in sauces, and the bright yellow flowers can be used to make many delicious dishes, such as dandelion omelette.

It should be noted that the stalks of the dandelions must be carefully discarded at all times. They contain a white juice which is slightly poisonous to people; so are the roots of the plant, unless roasted and ground as a coffee-substitute.

The flowers, however, contain no poisonous matter whatever, neither do the green or bleached leaves. The flowers can moreoever be used to make a cosmetic product, by boiling them in a little water for half an hour. The result is a liquid that is an excellent treatment for freckles and quite harmless to the skin.

## Dandelion Soup

1 cupful bleached dandelion leaves
1 tablespoonful of yellow dandelion petals
2 tablespoonsful butter or margarine
3 tablespoonsful flour
$\frac{1}{4}$ litre ($\frac{1}{2}$ pt.) water
$\frac{1}{2}$ litre (1 pt.) milk
salt
pepper
1 tablespoonful finely chopped chives
1 tablespoonful finely chopped parsley

Make a white sauce of the butter, the flour, the boiling milk and the water, stirring vigorously all the time until a smooth bound soup is made. Season with salt and pepper to taste and simmer for a few minutes. Pass the very finely chopped dandelion leaves through a sieve and add the liquid to the soup. Simmer for one minute, take off the ring and add the finely chopped chives, the parsley and the carefully removed dandelion petals.

Serve immediately, as hot as possible.

## Omelette with Dandelion Buds

4 eggs
4 tablespoonsful milk
salt
pepper
$\frac{1}{2}$ cupful dandelion buds
butter to fry

Pick the dandelion buds when they are still closed. Wash them carefully and gently stew them in the butter over low heat. The heat will open them slightly.

Beat the eggs with the milk, add salt and pepper to taste and pour the mixture over the slightly cooked buds. Cook as an ordinary omelette and serve on toast.

## Dandelion Cool Drink

½ litre (1 pt.) measure filled with dandelions
4 litres (7 pt.) water
4 lemons
2 kilos (4½ lb) sugar

Pick the flowers when they have just opened. Wash them
carefully and dry them. Pour the four litres of boiling
water onto the dried flowers. Leave this for twenty-four
hours, strain the liquid through a very fine cloth, add the
juice of the four lemons, as well as the grated rind of two
of the lemons. Finally add the sugar, put the pan back
over the fire and heat until all the sugar has been
dissolved, stirring all the time.

Strain everything through a sieve once more. Fill
carefully cleaned bottles with this drink, close carefully
and store in a cool, dark place. Serve this refreshing drink
with a little iced water or a few ice-cubes in tall glasses.

## Dandelion Wine

½ cupful raisins
½ litre (1 pt.) measure of dandelions
4 litres (7 pt.) water
2 oranges
1 lemon
15g (½ oz.) yeast
1½ kilos (2¼ lb) sugar

Pick the dandelions when they have just opened, wash
them and put them into a large pan. Bring them to the
boil with the four litres of water. Add the grated rind of
the oranges and the lemon, keep the juice for later use.
Add the sugar and leave to simmer for one hour. Pass
through a very fine sieve, leave the liquid to cool until it is
lukewarm. Then add the yeast. Leave for another
twenty-four hours. Add the orange and lemon juice, as
well as the raisins.

Pour the mixture into a large stoneware jar or a plastic bucket, cover it with a fine cloth to avoid dust, and leave it to ferment in a cool place for approximately three weeks.

Bottle this wine when the liquid has ceased to ferment.

## Dandelion Salad

**2 cupsful bleached dandelion leaves**
**2 tablespoonsful oil**
**1 tablespoonful vinegar**
**½ a small onion**
**salt**
**pepper**

Now that dandelions are the subject of discussion, the recipe of dandelion salad can hardly be left out. Bleach dandelion leaves by simply placing a brick over the young plants.

Look under the brick now and again to make sure that all is well and pick the leaves when they are nicely bleached and approximately ten centimetres long (four inches).

Proceed to make a salad in the ordinary way and garnish it with a few flowers. Discard the stalks, though, for the milky white juice is detrimental to our health.

# Elder

*Sambucus nigra*

A long time ago two young men lay down to rest in the shade of an old gnarled elder tree on a hot summer's day. They fell asleep and one of them had a strange dream. He dreamt that a little grey mouse crawled out of his companion's mouth. It stopped to look quickly around and then it hurried to the trunk of the old elder tree. It rummaged around for a while, rustling between the dead branches and dropped leaves. Suddenly it returned to the mouth of the sleeping young man as quickly as it had appeared.

When they woke up the young man told his friend of his curious dream. The latter was convinced that the dream had some kind of meaning, as dreams dreamt under an elder tree have prophetic powers.

'Let us take a closer look at the place where the mouse rummaged', he said, and together they started to feel the rough ground under the elder tree. There was no trace of a mouse-hole, but they did feel a hard cold object under the ground.

After some digging they unearthed a beautiful stoneware jar. When they finally managed to take the lid off the jar, it turned out to be filled to the very brim with gold and silver coins.

This old Pomeranian tale offers no explanations as to how the gold and silver came to be under the elder tree. Perhaps it was the treasure of a witch or a devil, for these are among the regular inhabitants of old elder trees.

This is the reason why these trees should be treated with some caution. Cutting one down or pulling one out is extremely risky, for the chances are that the devil will seek revenge for this enforced house-moving.

Should the inhabitant of the elder have been a witch instead of a devil the fate of the disturber of her peace is hardly better. The witch will strike all the chickens with illness and should the guileless human be naive enough to make a cradle out of the wood of the elder tree, the witch is certain to come and snatch any baby it contains. Fortunately the magic powers of the elder are not always turned against people, in fact, they favour them more often than not.

An elder tree planted next to the house will guard the inhabitants from all evil spirits and plagues. Perhaps the fact that elder keeps flies at a distance explains this tradition, as flies were and still are among the main carriers of disease.

In Switzerland fresh elder branches are hung in the windows and doors of the cheese dairy to prevent the souring of the milk and the cheese. In many other parts the farmers hang fresh elder branches in the doors of the stables and the living room.

A branch of an elder tree that grows on a pollard willow trunk is even more effective than an ordinary elder branch.

This particular type of elder has strong antidiabolical power and will protect everyone who wears a twig round the neck against all known evil.

In Syria people put their trust in the elderberry's anti-demonic powers, provided they are picked on midsummer's night and stored till Twelfth-night, 6 January. On that night the Devil roams around the house, but whoever draws a magic circle and stands in it with a handful of elderberries will come to no harm. The Devil will be powerless against him.

It is remarkable that all these stories of Devils and witches talk about the elder tree, its wood or its berries, but never of the elder blossom, with its delicate and sweet fragrance.

The elder blossom was and still is used in hot drinks to cure influenza and chase away a cold. In summer it is put into fritters and pancakes that in bygone days were meant for the empty stomachs of the reapers.

## Elder Blossom Fritters

**8 elder flowers**
**150g (5 oz.) plain flour**
**2 small eggs**
**¼ litre (½ pt.) milk**
**oil for frying**

Make a batter of the milk, the loosely beaten eggs and the flour.

Pick the elder flowers early in the morning when the dew has just dried, but pick only the umbels of which the outer flowers have fully opened.

Wash the flowers, dry them carefully and dip them into the batter one by one. Deep fry them in hot oil until they are golden brown, drain the fritters on greaseproof paper and serve them dusted with sugar and cinnamon.

They may also be served with a sauce made of two parts heated honey and one part cognac.

## Elder blossom Pancakes

**250g (9 oz.) self-raising flour**
**1 egg**
**4½ decilitre (16 fl.oz.) milk**
**a pinch of salt**
**butter**
**margarine or oil for frying**
**1 cupful elder blossom**

Pick fully blown umbels of elder blossom early in the morning. Place them in a basket, cover and leave it in a warm place for several hours. All the flowers on the umbels will open and can easily be shaken off.

Shake the blossoms into a clean white cloth and use a cupful of them in the pancake batter.

Make a batter of the milk, the loosely beaten egg and the self-raising flour, add the elder blossom and a pinch of salt. Make approximately twelve pancakes in the ordinary way, using butter, margarine or oil for frying.

Pile them up, keep them hot and serve hot with sugar and cinnamon, if desired.

## Elder Fritters from a Yeast Dough

**1 cupful elder blossom**
**250g (9 oz.) plain flour**
**1 egg**
**12g (¼ oz.) fresh yeast**
**2¼ decilitres (8 fl.oz.) milk**
**1 apple**
**salt**
**oil for frying**

Cover the fully blown elder blossom umbels and leave them in a warm place for several hours. All flowers will open and can easily be shaken off each umbel.

Shake the blossoms into a clean cloth and use a cupful of them in the fritter-dough.

Make the dough: sieve the flour into a large bowl, add the salt, make a depression in the middle of the flour and break the egg into it. Mix the yeast with part of the lukewarm milk and pour this into the depression as well. Finally add the remainder of the milk.

Cover with dough and leave to prove for approximately one hour.

Use two buttered tablespoons to form round fritters and deep-fry them in hot oil. Turn them once after approximately three minutes and continue to fry for another two minutes or until they are golden brown.

The fritters are cooked when a knitting needle can be inserted and comes out clean.

Drain the elder fritters and serve them hot sprinkled with sugar and cinnamon.

## Elder blossom Lemonade (8 glasses for immediate use)

**8 elder blossom umbels**
**4 lemons**
**100g (4 oz.) sugar**
**1½ litre (2½ pt.) water**

Place the carefully washed elder blossom umbels at the bottom of a large glass bowl and cover them with the sliced lemons. Add the sugar, dissolved in a little boiling water, and finally add the remainder of the water.

Cover and leave the mixture to draw for twenty-four hours. Strain and serve in cooled glasses.

## Cool milk-drink with Elder (4 glasses)

**½ litre (1 pt.) milk**
**2 cupsful elder blossom**
**3 eggs**
**1 cupful castor-sugar**
**cinnamon**

Simmer the milk and the elder blossom over low heat for

ten minutes. Strain the milk. Beat the egg-yolks and the sugar until they are frothy, add the milk to this mixture, whisking all the time.

Leave the drink in a cold place to cool. Loosely beat the egg-whites and whisk them into the milky drink just before serving.

Serve in tall glasses with a little cinnamon sprinkled on the top.

## Elder blossom Syrup

**750g (1¾ lb) sugar**
**250g (9 oz.) elder blossom**
**the grated skin and the juice of 2 lemons**
**½ litre (1 pt.) water**

Simmer the elder blossom in the water over low heat for fifteen minutes. Strain the fluid. Add the sugar, the lemon juice and the lemon peel to the elder blossom water and boil it until it becomes a syrup.

Pour the syrup into clean jam jars and seal. Elder blossom syrup is used to enhance the aroma of fruit salads and other fruit dishes with its light muscat-like taste.

## Elder blossom Champagne

This sparkling and delightfully fresh drink will be ready for drinking after two months.

**2 cupsful fully blown elder blossom**
**4 litres (7 pt.) water**
**1 lemon**
**750g (1¾ lb) sugar**
**¼ cupful white wine-vinegar**

Fill a large stoneware jar or a plastic bucket with the elder blossom umbels, of which the thickest stalks have been removed, the sliced lemon, the sugar, the vinegar and the cooled, boiled water.

Cover the container and leave it in a cool place for forty-eight hours. Strain and fill carefully cleaned bottles with the liquid. Cork the bottles and seal them with a little molten wax to ensure airtightness.

Store the bottles in a dark, cool place and leave them for two months, when the wine will be ready to drink. Fermentation will have formed a little carbon dioxide in the bottles, which gives this fresh summer drink its champagne like character.

# Hollyhocks

*Althea*

When the chief rabbi heard that a young woman by the name of Mary was to be mother to the Son of God, he called for a meeting with all the other rabbis.

They sat down together and discussed in what way they could best protect the young mother-to-be.

'She must have a man by her side to look after her and to protect her against slanderous tongues', said the priests.

'But he would have to be a very special young man. The mother to God's Son can hardly be entrusted to the first man we lay eyes on. We shall have to find her a good and strong husband, but how shall we ever successfully find one from the ranks of the ignorant and stubborn young men of today?' sighed the old rabbi.

The priests nodded soberly in agreement, they could not see the answer to the problem either.

Day and night they deliberated on this situation, but they failed to find a solution until the youngest of the rabbis, who had silently listened to all that was said, asked for permission to make a suggestion. The rabbis nodded.

The young rabbi got up and said, 'If the child of the young woman Mary is indeed the Son of God, we shall have to leave the choice of a husband to protect her to God as well. God will help us by giving us a sign'.

The rabbis looked at each other on hearing these words. Why had none of them thought of this earlier?

The chief rabbi agreed with relief and withdrew to the temple to pray. Then he had every young man and bachelor from miles around called to the temple.

The next day all the young and the not so very young bachelors were gathered at the temple. They were brimming with curiosity. What could the rabbi possibly want with them? When the last one had arrived, the chief rabbi told them that from their ranks a husband would be chosen for Mary, the young woman who was destined to give birth to the Son of God.

The men mumbled and whispered in amazement and many turned round to get away from the temple as quickly as they could. Finally only ten men remained. Young men who knew Mary and would be only too happy to look after her; and some older men who considered it an honour to be allowed to sue for the hand of the mother of God's Son.

But Mary herself, to the dismay of the men, was nowhere to be seen. They could not understand why the young woman, about whom all the fuss was, should remain hidden. Then the chief rabbi handed each of them an old gnarled stick and asked them to stand in a circle.

Somewhat taken aback, the young men complied with his request. As soon as they stood there in a circle the rabbi closed his eyes and prayed to God for a signal. When he opened his eyes he saw that a beautiful rose-red hollyhock had sprung from one of the dead sticks. At the same moment a dove flew down from the sky and settled on the stick. The stick was held by Joseph, a poor carpenter and the chief rabbi acknowledged that God had chosen this man to become Mary's husband.

This is one of the few legends in which the hollyhock

plays a part. This particular legend comes from Malta. In Malta, the hollyhock, which originally came from China, was known for many centuries before it became popular in the West. Though the hollyhock never became truly popular on the Continent, it was to become one of the most loved garden plants in England. In this country the hollyhock not only adorns practically every country cottage garden, but it is also used in a number of recipes to adorn the table.

There are even some recipes that enable people to see fairies. I have included such a recipe for any possible devotee. One never knows!

## Hollyhock Salad

**1 head of lettuce
1 cupful red hollyhock petals
3 tablespoonsful oil
2 tablespoonsful lemon juice
salt and pepper**

Carefully wash the lettuce and the hollyhock petals. Mix the washed and dried lettuce and hollyhock petals in a salad bowl.

Make a dressing of the oil, the lemon juice, the salt and the pepper and pour it over the pretty green and red salad just before serving. Garnish with a single red hollyhock flower, if desired.

## Salad with Hollyhock Buds

**2 cupsful hollyhock buds
3 tablespoonsful oil
2 tablespoonsful lemon juice
salt and pepper**

Pick the buds just before they open. Wash them carefully and place the buds in a saucepan with approximately 2 cm (just under 1 inch) of water.

Bring the water and the hollyhock buds to the boil. Cover and leave to simmer gently for three minutes.

Pour the buds into a colander and leave them to drain thoroughly. Make a dressing of the oil, the lemon juice, the salt and the pepper.

Pour this over the cooled hollyhock buds, and place in a salad bowl. Leave the salad for approximately one hour before serving, to allow the tastes to blend.

## Hollyhock Tea

**4 tablespoonsful dried hollyhock petals**
**1 litre (1¾ pt.) boiling water**

Pick the flowers of a dark red hollyhock before sunrise. Wash them and let them dry on a layer of absorbent kitchen paper.

When dry, pick off the petals, remove and discard possible white bits and leave the petals to dry thoroughly in a shady, airy place.

Store them in an airtight jar and use them to make an aromatic dark red tea.

# Lavender

*Lavendula officinalis*

Many centuries ago a beautiful young maiden was grazing her cows in the quiet, lonely Gail valley in Carinthia. As she sat down under a tree to rest awhile in its shade, a handsome young man dressed in green stood suddenly before her. He looked down at her with love-filled eyes and courteously asked if he might sit down with her and rest himself.

The young shepherdess hesitated before answering. Her life held little excitement and was very lonely, and the young man looked attractive and interesting.

She could not make up her mind and told him to come back the next day, but at an earlier hour, since milking-time was near.

The young man did not show his disappointment and promised to be back the next day at the arranged time. After bidding her a polite farewell, he turned around and went back into the forest. The maiden watched him go and saw that his back was hollow. She knew this to be a certain sign of the Devil in human appearance.

Frightened, she went to the village priest for help as soon as she returned home from the meadows. The priest advised her to delay the meeting with the Devil for one more day and to find out which plants he hated most.

The love-stricken Devil walked into her trap and

admitted to be deadly afraid of Lavender, Southernwood (*Artemisa abrotanum*) and Hairmoss (*Polytrichum*). On the way back to the village she picked a bouquet of these flowers, which the priest blessed for her.

The next day she hid the bouquet under a bush. She did not show the flowers until the Devil tried to seduce her. On seeing the bouquet of lavender the Devil disappeared amid a terrible roar of flames. Since that day, Lavender has been seen as an anti-demonic plant. Lavender is used not only to keep evil far from home, but also to fight many diseases.

St Hildegardis, a learned Benedictine abbess, dedicates a whole chapter to Lavender. She advises the use of antiseptic lavender oil as a healing agent for wounds and burns. Lavender oil is made by adding a handful of lavender flowers to oil and leaving it for three days, then replacing the old flowers by new ones, repeating this process as often as necessary to get a heavy lavender-scented oil. Lavender oil may also be successfully used against head-lice.

Lavender water, made of 5g lavender flowers left to draw in a litre of boiling water for five minutes, is refreshing and has a calming effect, according to the abbess, who also mentions the fact that lions are fond of lavender. Forewarned is forearmed! The use of lavender water does not originate in St Hildegardis's time. The Romans used lavender extract in their bathwater. In fact, the name is derived from the Latin *lavare* meaning to wash.

## Lavender Sugar

**250g (9 oz.) lavender flowers**
**750g (26 oz.) sugar**

Pick the flowers when they have just opened, preferably on a dry and sunny day.

Mix the flowers and the sugar in a mixer or mortar

until the mixture is smooth and even.

Fill air-tight jars with the sugar and use it to give a special flavour to fruit salads, cool drinks or flower teas.

After approximately one year the lavender sugar will have lost most of its aroma, but by then there will be new lavender flowers to replenish the stock.

## Lavender and Mint Jelly

**2 kilos (4½ lb) cooking apples**
**2 cupsful finely chopped mint leaves**
**½ cupful sugar**
**½ cupful water**
**½ cupful lavender flowers**

Cut the apples into quarters, but don't peel or core them. Put them into an enamel pan, just covered with water and bring them to the boil. Simmer gently for twenty minutes. The apples should then just be soft, but not yet cooked to a mash. Pour it all into a very fine sieve to leak through. Do not rub the apples through the sieve since this would render the jelly cloudy. Measure the jelly after half an hour. Usually about two and a half cups of apple juice will be the result. Exactly the same amount of sugar is added and the juice is heated to 100°C, but never higher than 105°C. Then the mint sauce is added. The mint sauce is made by leaving the finely chopped mint leaves in half a cup of sugar and a half a cup of water overnight.

Bring this mixture to the boil the following day. Leave the mint-sauce to cool, pass through a sieve and add the sauce to the warm apple jelly.

Place a few lavender flowers at the bottom of carefully cleaned jars and pour the warm jelly onto the flowers.

Cover the jars with cellophane and store in a dry cool place.

## Lavender Honey

**1 cupful fresh lavender flowers
1 jar of honey (500g 1 lb)**

Pour the honey into a saucepan and heat till it becomes liquid. Add the washed and dried lavender flowers and leave to simmer very gently for ten minutes. Take the saucepan from the stove, cover well and put away for twenty-four hours in a warm place.

Heat the honey and lavender flowers once more over a very low heat and pour the liquid mixture through a sieve. Store the lavender honey in tightly shut jars in a cool dry place, leaving for some time before use.

## Distilled Lavender Vinegar

**1 cupful fresh lavender flowers
$\frac{3}{4}$ litre (1$\frac{1}{2}$ pt.) wine-vinegar**

Fill an enamel tea kettle with the lavender flowers and the vinegar. Stop the spout with a cork, into which a hole has been made to tightly hold a piece of rubber hose. Fit a hose of approximately one metre into the cork. Guide the hose through a bucket or basin of cold water into a clean bottle. Bring the kettle to the boil and leave to boil gently over low heat. The steam will escape through the hose, will condense where the hose passes through the cold water and will end in the bottle as an aromatic liquid.

Use this lavender vinegar in fruit salads, pear-compote and in fruit drinks.

## Lavender and Pineapple Drink

**1 tin pineapple**
**1 litre (1¾ pt.) water**
**2 lemons**
**100g (4 oz.) sugar**
**2 teaspoonsful fresh lavender flowers and leaves**

Mix the cut-up pineapple, the pineapple juice, the water, the sugar and the juice of the two lemons. Leave the mixture to draw in a cool place for some time. Serve in glasses with a few lavender flowers and a single lavender leaf.

# Lilies

*Lilium candidum*

The 'lily of life' was known many centuries ago, a snow-white *Lilium candidum* laden with magic powers which sorcerers and their apprentices used for their games. The game of four Frankfurter sorcerers were brought to an abrupt end by Dr Faüst. He heard of these sorcerers while visiting Frankfurt and he decided to go and have a look. In the nearby market place he watched a Master sorcerer and three apprentice sorcerers play their macabre game in front of a large crowd of spectators. One by one the sorcerers chopped off each others head, in order to give it to the local barber. The barber was asked to shave the head and tidy the hair. Afterwards, the head was replaced on the neck of the decapitated sorcerer, who would then get up and be revived again, as if nothing had happened.

Dr Faust, however, who was a skilled sorcerer himself noticed what the watching crowd had failed to see. He saw four lilies of life placed under cover. The flower of one would bow to the earth when a head was chopped off, only to straighten again when the head was replaced. Faust understood that the strange powers of the lily were being mocked and abused, and decided to put an end to it.

When the Master Sorcerer's head was chopped off, Faust went into the corner where the lilies stood and cut through the stem of the wilting lily.

The other sorcerers had seen nothing and gaily continued the macabre game. They ordered the barber to shave and cut their master's hair with extra care. When he had finished, they replaced the head carelessly onto the neck of the victim. To their horror, the Master Sorcerer remained motionless. The crowd started bawling and shouting and the horrified apprentices fled and never returned to Frankfurt again.

This story illustrates the powers of the so-called 'lily of life'.

The way to obtain a lily of life is less macabre. For this purpose, a white lily must be picked between the twenty-third and the twenty-ninth of the month, when the sun is in the sign of the Lion, (Leo). This flower should then be kept under a mixture of barley and wheat for some time. When this has been accomplished, according to the rules, the lily will have magic powers that may be used for good or for evil.

A simpler version was to hang a flowering lily over the front door or a stable door to ward off all evil, as is done in England and Switzerland occasionally. Another spell was to make a draught of white lilies and flowering snapdragons, and to sponge the entire body with this liquid to maintain everlasting youth.

For the gourmets among us it would be useful to know that the young buds of the *Lilium Candidum* have a pleasant mild taste, provided they are picked before they are bigger than five centimetres, (two inches). Larger buds will taste a little sour and are best left unconsumed.

# Deep fried lily buds

**15 lily buds, no larger than 5 centimetres (2 inches)**
**40g (2½ oz.) sugar**
**100g & 4 oz.) self-raising flour**
**1½ decilitres (5 fl.oz.) milk**
**oil to deep fry**

Pick the lily buds when the dew has dried, wash them carefully, dry them and sprinkle them with the sugar. Make a batter of the self-raising flour and the milk, add a pinch of salt if wanted. Dip the lily buds into the batter one by one and quickly fry them brown in the hot oil. Let the excess oil leak off and serve hot with melted honey or sugar.

# Lily Honey

**2 white lily flowers**
**500g (18 oz.) honey**

Place the flowers in a stone jar, heat the honey and pour it over the flowers, when slightly cool. Leave for seven days. Heat the honey once more by placing the stone jar in a bowl of hot water.

Strain the honey when liquid and use it with sweet dishes.

# Lily Vinegar

**60g (2¼ oz.) dried flowers of the white lily**
**1 litre (1¾ pt.) vinegar**

Pour the vinegar onto the dried flowers. Keep this mixture in a clear glass jar or bottle and place in direct sunlight for fifteen days.

Strain and store this aromatic lily vinegar in a cool place.

# Marigolds

*Calendula officinalis*

For centuries the garden marigold was regarded as a medicinal herb and had to be satisfied with a small corner in the herb garden.

There it grew and flowered until someone got the idea to substitute the cheap dried marigold petals for the high-priced saffron. It was a very shrewd idea and soon the trade in 'saffron' was flourishing though not saffron made of the costly dried stigmas of an autumnal crocus, but of the dried petals of the marigold.

This trade increased so much that the authorities decided to check the swindle by introducing high fines for the sale of pseudo-saffron under the name of saffron. Meanwhile, however, many cooks and housewives had made the discovery that the medicinal marigold had many other qualities as well. The beautiful, sunny flower was moved from the herb-garden to the kitchen-garden and the decorative borders. Creative cooks began to experiment with the petals of the marigold, not only dried as a replacement for saffron, but also fresh from the garden.

It was a well-known fact by that time that the marigold was free of poison as well as aromatic and tasty. Especially in England the marigold was regarded highly by cooks and in the eighteenth century a midsummer dinner in marigold style became a country-wide tradition.

Not only was the table decoration of such a dinner made with marigolds, but each course had to have some marigold in it, from the hors d'oeuvre to the sweet.

Innumerable recipes were created at that time. The recipes that are still usable today and do not take too long to prepare have been included in this chapter. This is a challenge for those who would like to try their hand at a real marigold dinner.

In England, there were many uses of the marigold in the eighteenth century. Worried mothers brewed it into a drink together with thyme, rosemary and tansy.

On the 18 October, St Luke's day, the dried midsummer marigold, honey and wine, gave a good taste to this gold coloured brew and marriageable girls drank it on the evening of St Luke's day. They summoned St Luke to their aid with the words: 'St Luke, be kind to me and let me true love see'.

St Luke could hardly refuse such sweet summons. He was supposed to make the future husbands appear in the young girl's dream, so that she would know what her marriage prospects were.

This custom is almost certainly out of date, for emancipated women and Women's Libbers take a different view from the young girls in the eighteenth century when they choose their partners.

Maybe the taking of a marigold drink on the 18 October will become usual practice again when young men find out that they are in less demand. Why shouldn't St Luke give young men a helping hand as well?

In France, however, this custom will never become popular, for there the marigold flowers in midsummer and is seen as a symbol of middle age. In Mid-Europe it is even regarded as a symbol of jealousy.

The marigold is never used as an oracular flower, nor

are its sisters, the marguerite and the daisy. Young girls would be very unwise indeed to pull out the petals of the marigold one by one while reciting poems that either determine their future husband's profession or predict marriage, convent life, or spinsterhood. They know that the marigold is not suitable for this purpose, because bad luck and parting of lovers are brought about if the marigold's petals are pulled out during the recital of oracles.

So don't call on the magic powers of this flower, simply pull the petals out and use them either dried or fresh.

## Marigold Soup

**500g (18 oz.) potatoes**
**1 large onion**
**2 tablespoonsful finely chopped celery leaves**
**2 tablespoonsful finely chopped parsley**
**4 tablespoonsful marigold petals**
**2 tablespoonsful oil**
**½ litre (1 pt.) water**
**½ litre (1 pt.) milk**
**salt**
**pepper**
**1 tablespoonful flour**

Chop the peeled onion very small and fry in the oil in a large pan. Add the peeled potatoes chopped into small squares, the celery and one tablespoon of parsley. Leave to fry for a minute, then add enough water to just cover the vegetables. Leave to cook for 20 minutes over a low fire. Do not stir, for this might mash the potato-cubes.

Keep half cupful of milk back and add the rest of the milk to the vegetables after twenty minutes. Stir the flour and the remaining milk to a smooth paste and add this to the soup. Bring to the boil while stirring carefully, add the marigold petals and season with pepper and salt. Keep stirring until the soup thickens. Sprinkle the remaining parsley on top and serve piping hot with French bread.

## Potato Soufflé with Marigold Petals

**500g (18 oz.) potatoes**
**1 bay leaf**
**1½ cupsful milk**
**4 tablespoonsful butter or margarine**
**1 teaspoonful powder of marigold petals**
**2 eggs**
**1 tablespoonful fresh marigold petals**
**pepper**
**salt**

Peel the potatoes, cut small and cook them in a little salted water with the bay leaf. Pour the water off when they are done, allow them to steam dry and pass through a sieve. Meanwhile, heat the milk in a saucepan, add the butter and the powdered marigold petals, and stir this mixture into the hot potato *purée*. Season with salt and pepper.

Lightly beat the egg-yolks and stir into the potato mixture. Beat the egg whites very stiff and gently fold into the potato *purée*.

Butter an oven-proof dish, fill it with the potato *purée* and heat and brown in a pre-heated oven of approximately 200°C.

Decorate with the fresh marigold petals and serve hot.

## Carrots with Almonds and Marigold Petals

**1 lb carrots**
**1 cupful marigold butter**
**2 tablespoonsful chopped roast almonds**
**salt**
**pepper**
**½ teaspoonful powdered marigold petals**
**1 teaspoonful lemon juice**

Scrape the carrots and cook them in a little water. Add the marigold butter and when this has melted, add the roast almonds.

Mix the dry marigold petals with the lemon juice, and pour this mixture over the carrots. Leave to cook for five minutes over very low heat and serve hot.

## Sweet Marigold Rice

**½ cupful pudding-rice**
**4 cupsful milk**
**½ cupful sugar**
**2 tablespoonsful marigold petals**
**3 tablespoonsful cornflour**

Heat the milk with one tablespoon of fresh marigold petals. Add the rice and cook until the rice is done, stirring occasionally. Thicken the milk rice with the cornflour dissolved in a little milk. Add the sugar.

Place a few marigold petals at the bottom of four pudding dishes. Pour on the hot rice pudding and allow to cool. Turn the individual puddings onto plates before serving.

## Sweet Marigold Sauce

**1 egg**
**1 cupful butter or margarine**
**1 cupful sugar**
**½ teaspoonful lemon juice**
**some grated lemon skin**
**1 cupful marigold petals**

Stir the butter until soft and creamy, add the sugar and the egg and keep on stirring until the mixture is smooth. Add the marigold petals and the juice and grated lemon skin and heat in a double boiler with enough hot water to get a thick sauce.

Serve hot with baked custard or vanilla ice cream.

## Sugar Syrup with Marigold Petals

**750g (26 oz.) sugar**
**250g (9 oz.) marigold petals**
**juice and grated skin of 2 lemons**
**½ litre (1 pt.) water**

Mix all ingredients, put them into a thick-bottomed saucepan and leave it to boil until it is thin and syrup-like. Stir continuously to avoid burning and browning the syrup.

Pour into well cleaned jars. Cover with cellophane and store in a dry, cool place.

# Nasturtiums

*Tropaeolum Majus*

Nasturtium or Indian cress owes its name to the fact that the taste of the beautiful round leaves is very similar to that of Watercress and ordinary Garden cress, though there is absolutely no family relation. The smell as well as the scent of the nasturtium and the rape-seed-like water and garden cress are indeed so similar that even the cabbage butterfly, or cabbage-white gets confused. Very often they lay their eggs on the nasturtium plant and the caterpillars that emerge from the eggs hardly mind the mistake. They are quite happy to substitute nasturtium leaves for cabbage leaves.

This may explain the name of cress for the nasturtium, the 'Indian' part of it is harder to account for. It should probably be seen as an ignorant joke of people who considered everything foreign to have come from the East or West Indies. The latter does seem a more likely possibility, for as far as we know, Indian cress does come from South America, more specifically from Peru and did not get imported into Europe until the seventeenth century.

Since that time it has certainly become one of the gardener's favourite flowers.

The name nasturtium is also derived from its

similarity to water and garden cress. Nasturtium is a distortion of the Latin words *nasus tortus*, indicating the way some people turn up their noses while chewing the sharp tasting leaves of garden cress.

The leaves of the nasturtium may be chewed equally well and this is indeed still done in its country of origin, during long marches. The essential oils of the plant are said to have a cooling effect on the marchers.

In South America, many dishes are made with the leaves, the seeds and the flowers of the nasturtium, though it is mainly grown as a decorative plant. It forms an excellent defence against spiderfly, when planted under apple trees. A number of very tasty recipes for nasturtium dishes are included in this chapter.

Try adding a few capers of nasturtium (see recipe) to a glass of ice-cooled white vermouth (martini). Likewise, the use of a mixture of curd cheese, raisins and nuts rolled into a leaf of the *tropaeolum* as a tasty snack with drinks.

## Nasturtium with Gervais Cheese

**12 Nasturtium flowers**
**150g (5 oz.) Gervais or curd cheese**
**2 tablespoonsful fresh double cream**
**½ lemon**
**1 small onion**
**2 tablespoonsful mayonaise**
**1 tablespoonful finely chopped nasturtium leaf**
**salt**
**pepper**

Pick the flowers in the morning as soon as the dew has dried and keep them in a cool place.

Mix the Gervais or curd cheese with the double cream and the mayonnaise, seasoned with the juice of half a lemon, the very finely chopped onion, salt, pepper and the equally finely chopped nasturtium leaves.

Very carefully fill the flowers with this mixture just before serving, and try to avoid damaging them. Serve them as an *entrée* on a bed of freshly picked nasturtium leaves.

## Nasturtium Salad

**4 cupsful freshly picked nasturtium flowers**
**½ cupful nasturtium leaves**
**2 tablespoonsful finely chopped chervil**
**1 clove of garlic**
**2 tablespoonsful lemon juice**
**3 tablespoonsful oil**
**salt and pepper**

Wash the freshly picked nasturtium leaves and flowers carefully and leave them to dry on absorbent kitchen paper.

Make a dressing of the oil, lemon juice (or vinegar), salt, pepper and the finely chopped clove of garlic.

Gently mix the washed and dried nasturtium leaves and flowers with the finely chopped chervil in a salad bowl.

Pour the dressing over the salad and serve immediately.

## Nasturtium with Eggs

**12 fresh nasturtium flowers**
**½ cupful nasturtium leaves**
**4 hard-boiled eggs**
**1 tablespoonful finely chopped parsley**
**2 tablespoonsful mayonnaise**
**2 tablespoonsful oil**
**1 tablespoonful vinegar**
**salt**
**pepper**

Wash the nasturtium flowers carefully and leave them to

dry on absorbent kitchen paper.

Meanwhile, make a mixture of the mashed eggs, the finely chopped parsley, and the mayonnaise. Season to taste with salt and pepper. Fill the flowers with the mixture. Line the salad bowl with the washed and dried leaves of the nasturtium. Sprinkle them with a mixture of the oil, the vinegar and salt and pepper. Arrange the filled flowers on top and serve immediately.

## Capers of Nasturtium

**1 jamjar filled with nasturtium-seeds**
**2 bay leaves**
**1 teaspoonful dill seed**
**1 tablespoonful chopped horseradish**
**½ litre (1 pt.) vinegar**
**1 small onion**
**20g (¾ oz.) salt**
**1 teaspoonful peppercorns**

Pick the nasturtium seeds between three and seven days after the flower has dropped off. If they are picked later the taste will be seriously affected.

Layer the washed and dried seeds, some snippets of bay leaf, the horseradish and the dill-seed into a cleaned jamjar.

Bring the vinegar to the boil with the sliced onion, peppercorns and salt, simmer for ten minutes and allow to cool. When cold, pour this aromatic for ten minutes and allow to cool. When cold, pour this aromatic vinegar over the nasturtium seeds. Make certain that the seeds are completely covered. Cover the jars with cellophane paper and store in a dark, cool place for at least eight weeks.
* Use these capers to season sauces, soups, and salads.

# Peonies

*Peony*

It was the custom in the central part of the Netherlands, between the big rivers that cut it in half, for the local people to hang a peony-plant by a single thread from the ceiling at Whitsun. If the plant continued to grow the people of that house could count on good luck and prosperity for the year to come. However, if the plant died, they should be prepared for misfortune.

This custom is easily understood when one realises that the peony was counted among the magic plants. It was a plant that witches used to perpetrate their rare good deeds.

The fact that the seeds of the peony 'twinkle like stars in the night' according to Dodeonaeus, may have helped to attribute magic powers to this beautiful summer-plant.

These powers are, in fact, so important that the peony was given a special protector, the woodpecker. He watches over the plant from dawn to dusk and woe be to the man who dares to pick a peony or pull out the plant during the day time. The woodpecker will come rushing down to peck out his eyes.

That is the reason why peonies should always be picked in the dusk and the plant transplanted only by night. Even safer would be to push a stick among the roots in the daytime and to tie a strong rope to the stick. Then the rope is fastened to a dog's collar at dusk and the dog lured away from the spot with a piece of roast beef. The plant will be pulled out without making the woodpecker suspicious.

A few roots should be cut off before replanting the peony as they will protect the bearer against epilepsy. Moreover, even a few peony pips carried on the person will protect him against misfortune and disease. These magic forces will be even stronger when the pips and roots of the peony are harvested during the waning of the moon, before sun rise and in the dog days, that is the hottest part of the year in July and August, variously dated with reference to the rising of Sirius, the chief star in the Greater Dog.

To enjoy the healing powers of the peony as well as the taste of a delicious wine, leave fifteen peony pips in a litre of wine for a fortnight in a sunny place. The wine will not only become saturated with a very fine aroma but will also guard the drinker from nightmares and drunken stupor.

## Stewed Peonies

**4 red peony flowers**
**½ onion**
**1 clove garlic**
**2 tablespoonsful finely chopped parsley**
**2 tablespoonsful vinegar**
**water**
**salt**

Stew the washed peonies in a little salted water for a few minutes. Strain them well, place them in a heat-proof dish and keep them warm.

Chop the onion very small, press the clove of garlic, mix the finely chopped onion with the parsley, the vinegar and the garlic-juice and pour this mixture over the warm peonies.

Serve this seventeenth century recipe hot.

## Peony Syrup

**500g (18 oz.) peony flowers, preferably dark red ones**
**1½ decilitre (5 fl.oz.) water**
**1,500g (3½ lb) sugar**

Bring the water nearly to the boil and pour it over the washed peony blossoms.

Leave the mixture overnight, bring it to the boil and strain it.

Should the red liquid not be aromatic enough, a further 500g (18 oz.) of peonies should be picked, left to draw in the liquid, brought to the boil again and strained once more. The scent of the flowers depends mainly on the soil in which they are grown and on the weather conditions.

Once the draught is fragrant enough, the sugar is added and everything is boiled until it has a syrup-like consistency.

## Peony Water

**1,000g (2¼ lb) peony flowers**
**1 litre (1¾ pt.) water**
**1 litre (1¾ pt.) wine**

Leave the washed flowers to soak overnight in the wine. Remove the flowers from the wine, fill a kettle with the flowers and a litre fresh water. Make certain that the kettle can be tightly closed with a cork; make a hole in the cork and fit a piece of hose pipe of approximately 1.5 metres into the hole.

Lead the hose pipe through a bowl of cold water and finally into a bottle or glass jar.

Bring the water and the flowers to the boil. The steam will escape via the length of hose pipe, cool down in the bowl filled with cold water and finally drip into the bottle. This peony water, sweetened with honey to taste if wanted, was one of the refined delicacies of the seventeenth and eighteenth centuries.

# Primroses

*Primula veris*

The Druids, the magicians of the ancient Celts, were not only responsible for the upbringing and education of promising young Celts, as well as the administration of justice, they were also supposed to be able to predict the future.

In order to obtain this gift they brewed a magic potion at certain set times, called 'the juice of the revelation of the knowledge'.

To make this brew, primroses, cranberry flowers, grains of wheat and verbena flowers were picked by the new moon, boiled in a cauldron for a year and a day, over a fire lit by the breath of nine maiden Druids. Three drops of the boiling hot fluid were dropped onto the finger of a novice, and as he put his burned finger in his mouth, this was expected to give him the ability to predict the future.

In this particular old story, primroses play an important part, and in many stories to follow the primrose will be allocated many magic powers.

The resemblance of a bunch of primroses to a ring of keys is common in the myths and legends in which primroses give entry to underground treasure-chambers. To illustrate this let me tell you the story of a poor

herdsman in Swabia who gaily stuck a bunch of primroses in his hat. He walked and whistled happily and slowly it occured to him that his hat was growing heavier and heavier all the time, until he could no longer keep his head upright. He took off his hat and was very surprised to see that the lovely yellow flowers had changed into a very heavy ring of silver keys.

The cowherd took the keys in his hands, wondering what to do with them, when he heard the voice of a beautiful young maiden. She revealed to him that these silver keys would help him to unlock the hidden treasures in the Heuchel mountain.

'Once you have entered the mountain you must take care not to forget the most important thing', the maiden warned.

The cowherd hardly listened to her warning in his great excitement to have the legendary treasures within his reach.

He hurried away and with the help of his silver keys he opened a narrow crevice in the mountain. Once inside the mountain he could hardly believe his eyes. Never in his life had he seen so much gold, silver, and so many precious stones.

Hastily and greedily he filled his pockets until they could hold no more. However, the silver keys were carelessly left behind. As soon as he crawled through the small crevice out into the open again, he forget who he was and where he lived. This amnesia was the price of his folly and he was doomed to wander for the rest of his life.

In Dutch and German the primrose is commonly called 'the key flower', a name which is easily understood in connection with these legends. It is also called 'pancake flower'.

For many centuries the primrose was held in high esteem for its delicate aniseed-like flavour in desserts and pancakes. The custom to add primrose flowers to the pancake batter has survived to this day.

In the eighteenth century the primrose became so popular in the kitchen that serving primrose pudding or primrose cake became the last word in refined hospitality. Obviously this custom was restricted to Spring, as the primrose is one of our loveliest messengers of Springtime. The Latin name of this pretty wild flower is connected with its time of flowering and is derived from *primus*, meaning first, and *ver* meaning Spring. The English name 'primrose' is in fact derived from a similar source, namely *prima rosa* meaning first rose.

## Salad with Primroses

**1 head of lettuce**
**1 cucumber**
**½ cupful primrose buds picked just before they open**
**½ cupful green olives**
**¼ cupful shredded almonds**
**4 tablespoonsful oil**
**2 tablespoonsful vinegar**
**½ tablespoonsful water mint leaves**
**salt and pepper**

Wash the lettuce and drain. Peel the cucumber and slice very thinly. Halve the olives and remove the stones. Shred the almonds.

Cover the bottom of the salad bowl with the lettuce leaves, and place a mixture of sliced cucumber, the washed primrose buds, the halved, de-stoned olives and the shredded almonds on top of the lettuce bed.

Mix the oil with the vinegar, the salt and the pepper and pour this dressing over the salad.

Mix all ingredients very lightly and leave the salad in a cool place for a quarter of an hour to enable the various tastes to blend.

Garnish the salad with a few leaves of water mint just before serving.

## Primrose Pancakes (10 to 12)

200g (7 oz.) flour
2 eggs
½ litre (1 pt.) milk
½ cupful yellow primroses
salt
butter or margarine to fry

Make a batter of the flour, the lightly beaten eggs, some salt and the milk. Sprinkle the washed and dried primrose flowers into the batter and make pancakes in the usual way.

## Primrose Cake

100g (4 oz.) butter or margarine
135g (4½ oz.) sugar
75g (3 oz.) flour
75g (3 oz.) self-raising flour
salt
½ cupful yellow primroses

Pick the primroses dew-fresh, wash them and leave them to dry on absorbent kitchen paper.

Stir the butter until it is creamy, add the eggs and the sugar and continue to stir until the mixture is nice and frothy.

Add the mixture of the flour and the self-raising flour, spoonful by spoonful, beating vigorously all the time. Finally fold the primroses into the batter. They will give the cake a delicate aroma and taste.

Fill a buttered cake tin for two-thirds with the batter and bake it like an ordinary cake for one and a half hours at 150°C.

Turn the cake after cooling for a few minutes onto a cake-rack.

Leave to cool and garnish with crystalized primroses (see recipe) if desired.

## Primrose Pickle

**1 cupful freshly picked primroses of all colours**
**1 cupful sugar**
**1 cupful vinegar**

Fill a clean jamjar with the washed and dried primroses. Boil the vinegar and the sugar till it becomes a syrupy liquid, and pour this syrup, when cooled, over the flowers.

Seal the jar with cellophane paper and store in a cool dark place before use.

## Crystalized Primroses

**1 cupful freshly picked yellow primroses**
**1 cupful sugar**
**a little water**

Pick the primroses when the dew has dried. Clean them very carefully. Boil the sugar and a little water until it becomes a syrup.

Remove the syrup from the heat and dip in the primroses one by one. Let the crystalized flowers dry on a piece of aluminium foil, turning them carefully once to make certain that they dry equally well on all sides.

Store the crystalized flowers in a tightly sealed jar, when they have thoroughly dried.

Keep them in a dry, cool place and use them to decorate cakes and puddings.

# Roses

*Rosa*

The forester's wife was young and extremely pretty. Her hair was scented like a flower-field in June and her eyes shone like blue gentian bells.

Her husband was a good man, but poor. In fact, he was so poor that there was not even enough money to buy furniture, let alone pretty clothes for his young wife. The young woman knew this and found comfort in the pretty flowers of the field that grew at the edge of the forest. She picked armfuls of them each day to beautify her home and herself with their gay colours and lovely fragrance. In search of new treasures she came upon a rose bush in full flower one day, growing on a heap of stones. She walked towards it, but suddenly stopped in her tracks.

Next to the rose bush stood suddenly a gnome, a little man in yellow boots. The little man beckoned her to come nearer but the young woman became frightened and ran away. She ran home to escape from the flowering rose bush and the little man.

The following day, when her husband had gone out to work again, she had lost her fright and curiosity got the better of her. She set out to find the flowering rose bush once more.

To her dismay she discovered that the rose bush had been pulled up. The heap of stones and a small purse with silver money were all that remained.

She quickly gathered up the purse and hid it under her apron. She ran home with it and put the money away under a loose floor-board.

When her husband came home she kept her discovery to herself. The next day she went back to the spot where the rose bush had flowered. Once more she found a purse full of silver and once more she hid it under the floorboard when she came home.

This continued for eleven days, but on the twelfth day the forester got home unexpectedly early and found his young wife bent over her newly acquired treasure. He became suspicious as to the source of the money and asked her about it. She promptly told him the whole story about the rose bush, the little man and the money.

'Well', said the husband, 'If that is so, I would like to see it for myself', and the next morning he accompanied his wife to the place where once the rose bush had flowered.

But, alas, there was neither a rose bush, nor a little man, nor a purse of money.

This story is just one of the innumerable legends and myths that have been woven around the rose.

The rose has inspired many a poet and artist to make works of art that have defied the centuries, but the most fascinating of them all is a poem written by Gertrude Stein. She wrote in a circle:

A rose is a rose is a rose is a rose ...

This poem is the best illustration of the timelessness of the rose, this wonderful flower which adorned the hanging gardens of Babylon by the thousands. At a rough estimate there are known to be thirty thousand varieties today, all of them bred from the one hundred and fifty botanic strains that are spread over the Northern hemisphere.

The cross-breeding of botanic roses to create new ones that are even more beautiful and sweeter scented was practised as early as 300 B.C. by the Chinese. Excavations in Crete reveal that an extensive rose culture existed on the island in 1600 B.C. The Romans simply idolized the rose; their love grew into a true rose cult. There are said to be some Roman Emperors who could only sleep on a bed of freshly-picked rose petals and history claims that the beautiful Cleopatra received Marcus Aurelius in a hall covered with a two inch thick carpet of fresh rose petals.

The love of the rose was not restricted to the admiration of its transient beauty and colour. The Romans were also well aware of its culinary possibilities. Nero's favourite dish is said to have been rose pudding.

It is hardly surprising that the rose, that played such an important part in the life of the Romans, was totally rejected by the early Christians as a symbol of heathen waste and exuberance. It played no part in their church. But, a rose is a rose is a rose; so as time went by the rose was once more restored to her old glory as the queen of flowers. This happened because someone related her five crown-leaves with the five wounds of Christ!

In the course of the Middle Ages we see the rose reappear as part five of Christian symbolism. It was also in the Middle Ages that experiments were once again carried out on the rose as a cosmetic aid and as a basic ingredient for aromatic, usually sweet, dishes.

In all these dishes, a great many of which have been included in this chapter, only fully grown, scented roses are used, picked in the early morning when the dew has just dried. The best qualities of the rose, as indeed of any flower, will then be captured.

## Filled Eggs with Rose Petals

Choose scented rose petals for this recipe, preferably soft yellow or orange in colour, since these colours will blend better with the yellow of the egg-yolk.

**8 hard-boiled eggs**
**2 tablespoonsful mayonnaise**
**1 tablespoonful lemon juice**
**1 teaspoonful dried powdered rose petals**
**1 teaspoonful finely chopped onion**
**1 teaspoonful salt**
**1 teaspoonful sugar**
**$\frac{1}{4}$ teaspoonful pepper**
**$\frac{1}{2}$ cupful fresh finely chopped rose petals**

Peel the hard-boiled eggs, cut them in half and very carefully remove the yolks. Place the whites on a plate, on a few leaves of lettuce if desired.

Mix the mashed yolks with the mayonnaise, the herbs and spices and the lemon juice, using either a fork or a mixer. Whisk the mixture until it is smooth and light. Fill the whites of the eggs with the mixture, preferably using an icing-set.

Garnish with the finely chopped fresh rose-petals just before serving.

## Rose and Cheese Dish

**3 eggs**
**1 cupful milk**
**1 cupful breadcrumbs**
**2 tablespoonsful butter**
**$\frac{1}{2}$ teaspoonful salt**
**1 teaspoonful rosewater**
**$1\frac{1}{2}$ cupsful grated mature or Parmesan cheese**
**1 cupful crystalized rose petals**

Heat the milk to a temperature of approximately 40°C. Separate the eggs and whisk the yolks into the warmed milk. Add the breadcrumbs, the cheese, the butter, the salt and the rose water and place a bowl containing this mixture in a panful of boiling water. Heat the mixture in this double boiler and stir continually until it has thickened.

Allow the mixture to cool, stirring all the time. Preheat the oven at 175°C.

Beat the egg-whites till very stiff, gently fold them into the mixture of egg-yolks, cheese and breadcrumbs. Fill a buttered ovenproof dish with this mixture, place the dish in the middle of the oven and leave to cook for approximately fifty minutes. Place the crystalized rose petals on the top and return the dish to the oven for an additional five minutes. Serve as hot as possible.

The way to prepare crystalized rose petals can be found in the chapter on *General ways of preparing flowers*. (*Page 11*)

## Apple and Rose Dish

**6 large cooking-apples, preferably Bramleys**
**1/3 cupful sugar**
**1 tablespoonful white wine (or dry sherry)**
**1½ teaspoonsful rosewater**
**¼ teaspoon cinnamon**
**a generous pinch ground cloves**
**3 tablespoonsful butter**
**2 large eggs**
**a pinch of salt**
**¼ teaspoonful baking-powder**
**1 cupful crystalized rose petals**

Peel the apples, quarter and core them. Cook them gently in the wine (or sherry), the sugar, the rose water and the spices till they are done. Pass the apples and spices through a sieve, pour the *purée* into a bowl and whisk the egg yolks into the apple sauce. Place the bowl into a pan of boiling water and continue to whisk until the apple and egg mixture starts to thicken.

Pour the thickened mixture into an ovenware dish and cook in a pre-heated oven of approximately 175°C for twenty to twenty-five minutes.

Beat the egg whites, the water, the salt and the baking powder until it is very stiff. Finally beat the sugar into the stiff egg whites. Cover the apple dish with the beaten egg whites, gently fold in a few rose petals and return the dish to the oven until the egg whites have become golden brown.

Serve as hot as possible.

## Hot Rose and Chocolate Sauce

$\frac{1}{2}$ cupful water
100g (4 oz.) dark chocolate (cooking chocolate)
1 cupful sugar
$\frac{1}{4}$ teaspoonful salt
1 tablespoonful butter
1 teaspoonful distilled rose water

Bring the water to the boil in a small sauce pan. Add the broken chocolate and keep stirring until it has melted. Add the sugar and the salt. Keep stirring until the sugar and salt have dissolved and leave the mixture to simmer for five minutes. Add the butter and the rose water and serve this aromatic chocolate sauce piping-hot with vanilla ice-cream, cold custard or cold semolina pudding.

The recipe for distilled rose water can be found in the chapter on *General ways of Preparing Flowers*. (*Page 11*)

## Rose Petal Jam

500g (1$\frac{1}{4}$ lb) red rose petals
850g (2 lb) sugar
$\frac{1}{2}$ cupful water
2 tablespoonsful lemon juice

Use scented dark red roses for this jam. Pick the petals,

remove the white lower parts of the petals carefully, wash them and dry them with care. Fill a thick-bottomed pan with layers of rose petals and sugar. Add the water and the lemon juice, bring the mixture slowly to the boil, cover and simmer gently for ten minutes. Stir occasionally to prevent burning.

After approximately ten minutes remove the lid, take a teaspoonful of the mixture and allow a few drops to fall onto the cold working top. If it forms a little ball, the jam is ready, if not, simmer for a few more minutes.

Fill carefully cleaned air-tight jamjars with the rose jam, seal them and store them in a dry, cool place.

## Rose Honey I

**250g (9 oz.) red rose petals**
**2 kilos (4½ lb) honey**
**1½ litres (2¾ pt.) water**

Use scented red roses for the making of rose honey. Wash the petals, after discarding the white lower parts of the petals. Dry them carefully before pouring the one and a half litres of boiling water onto them. Leave this mixture in a cool place, covered against dust, for at least twelve hours.

Pass everything through a sieve and add this rose juice to the honey. Simmer the honey and rose juice over very low heat until it has the normal consistency of honey once again. Fill clean jamjars with this beautifully coloured honey.

## Rose Honey II

**1 cup rose petals**
**1 jar honey 500g (1¼ lb)**

Wash the rose petals and remove the white lower ends of the petals. Heat the honey in a thick-bottomed pan, add rose petals and simmer over very low heat for ten minutes.

Leave the pan in a cool place for 24 hours. Re-heat the honey and pass the hot honey and rose petal mixture through a sieve.

Fill clean jam jars with the scented honey. If desired the honey can be left unstrained and eaten with the rose petals still in it.

## Crystalized Rose Petals

**1 cupful rose petals**
**2 egg whites**
**1 cupful white sugar**

Dry the washed rose petals very carefully and paint them one by one with the egg white, whisked lightly with a little sugar. Coat the egg-covered rose petals with sugar. Let the sugared petals dry for a little while on a plate covered with absorbent kitchen paper.

Cover the petals with the lightly beaten egg white once more, using a paint-brush to make the job easier. Coat the petals in sugar again and leave them to dry thoroughly in a very moderate oven, better still in the sunshine.

Turn them over once during the drying process.

When the petals feel completely dry and brittle, layer and store them in an airtight tin.

Use these beautiful crystalized rose petals to decorate cakes and puddings.

## Rose Scented Carrots

**500g (1¼ lb) young, tender carrots**
**½ cupful rose butter**
**1/3 cupful rose sugar**
**1 tablespoonful chopped mint leaves**

Wash the carrots and scrape them carefully. Cook them in a little water for approximately twenty minutes until they are done. Pour off the excess water. Melt the rose butter in a separate saucepan and add the rose sugar. When the butter and sugar are properly melted pour the mixture over the carrots or add the carrots to the butter-sugar mixture and heat them again. After simmering for five minutes remove the carrots from the heat, add the finely chopped mint leaves, mix everything well. Serve hot.

## Rose Pickles

**250g (9 oz.) rose buds**
**250g (9 oz.) sugar**
**½ litre (1 pt.) white wine-vinegar**

Pick the rose buds when they are still completely green. Place a layer of washed rose buds in a stoneware jar, sprinkle generously with sugar, place another layer of rose buds on top, sugar again until all the rose buds and the sugar have been used. Bring the wine-vinegar to the boil, leave it to cool before pouring it over the layered rose buds and sugar.

Cover the jar and leave in a cool place. Use these pickled rose buds as soon as they are tender and aromatic, but do not keep them too long as they are perishable.

## Rose Biscuits with caraway-seed

**350g (12 oz.) plain flour**
**250g (9 oz.) butter or margarine**
**250g (9 oz.) castor sugar**
**1 teaspoonful ground nutmeg**
**2 teaspoonsful caraway seed**
**3 teaspoonsful rose water**

Stir the butter until it is creamy, add the sugar and the rose water drop by drop. Finally add the ground nutmeg and the caraway seeds. Knead the flour into the mixture and leave the dough in the refrigerator or a cool place to stiffen. Roll it out until it is $\frac{1}{2}$ cm ($1\frac{1}{4}$ inch) thick and cut into round shapes with a biscuit cutter (or a small glass), or cut the dough into diamond shapes. Place the biscuits on a buttered baking sheet and bake them in a warm oven (160°C) for fifteen to twenty minutes until they are golden brown.

### Rose Petal Tea

**2 cupsful freshly picked petals of dark red roses**
**1 litre ($1\frac{3}{4}$ pt.) water**
**honey**

Pick the roses as soon as the dew has dried, wash the petals, remove and discard the white lower parts and place the petals in a teapot.

Pour the boiling water into the teapot and leave the rose tea to brew for ten minutes.

Serve this tea hot or iced, with honey to enhance the delicate taste.

# Sunflowers

*Helianthus annuus*

The bright golden colour and the shape of the sunflower resemble old pictures of the Sun. The sunflower owes its name to this resemblance. Strangely enough, the association with this important celestial body, has failed to weave a net of legends and myths around the sunflower. The sunflower plays no part in European folklore, at all. That is hardly surprising, however, for the sunflower was unknown in Europe until after the discovery of America.

In the course of the sixteenth century the sunflower was introduced into Europe from America together with many other plants such as the potato, the tomato and the green (haricot) bean. But it was some time before this giant among the annual summer plants, which easily grows to eight foot and more, became truly popular.

Today sunflowers are grown everywhere, as a decorative flower, as a windbreak in private gardens and as a commercial crop. In the latter case they are grown for the seeds, which are rich in oil with a high percentage of polyunsaturated fats. The oil is used to make salad oils and diet margarine.

There are many more possibilities for the use of the kernels as well as the green buds of the sunflower, as the following recipes show.

## Sunflower Buds with Butter Sauce

**4 cupsful fresh green sunflower buds**
**½ cupful butter**
**3 tablespoonsful lemon juice**
**2 tablespoonsful finely chopped garden mint**
**salt and pepper**

Pick the sunflower buds when they are still closed and green. Wash them carefully and leave them to dry.

Cover the bottom of a large saucepan with approximately three centimetres of water (just over one inch). Add a teaspoon of salt, bring the water to the boil, turn the heat down and gently slide the sunflower buds into the boiling water. Cover the saucepan and gently simmer the buds until they are done. This will usually take about fifteen minutes.

Strain the buds and drain them well. Place them on a flat serving plate and keep them hot.

Melt the butter in a thick-bottomed saucepan, but do not brown it.

Add the lemon juice, the finely chopped mint and the salt and pepper, stirring all the time.

Pour this fragrant herb butter over the cooked sunflower buds and serve immediately.

## Biscuits with Sunflower Kernels

**¼ cupful fresh sunflower seeds, husked and cleaned**
**½ cupful butter**
**½ cupful Demerara sugar**
**1 egg**
**1½ cupsful self-raising flour**
**1 packet vanilla sugar**
**a pinch of salt**

Stir the butter until creamy and add the egg. Continue to stir until the mixture is light and frothy. Add the vanilla sugar and the Demerara sugar. Keep stirring until the sugar has dissolved.

Fold in the sieved flour and the sunflower kernels. Use two teaspoons to form little heaps of dough and place them on a buttered baking sheet.

Pre-heat the oven at 200°C, place the biscuits in the oven and cook them for approximately ten minutes or until they are golden-brown.

# Tansy

*Tanacetum Vulgare*

On midsummer's night, an old farmer from Brodwin in
Germany rode to town with his wife to get beer for the
approaching midsummer-festivities.

It had been a dry, hot day and the sand was so loose
that the horses made little progress. The farmer took pity
on the poor creatures and stepped down from the cart to
make the going easier.

With the reins in hand he walked beside the cart and
gently encouraged his horses.

His wife stayed on the cart and dropped off to sleep.
When she woke up, she called out to her husband. He
answered, but the farmer's wife could not see him,
though the moon shone brightly in the summer night. All
she could see were the reins, which seemed to be held by
an invisible hand. She took fright and called her
husband's name several times. He answered her each
time but remained invisible.

Then the woman understand that magic powers had
been at work and together they decided to get to town as
fast as possible. There they might find someone who
could undo the magic spell.

They stopped at the first inn and the woman told their
story to the innkeeper, who showed no surprise at all. He
seemed familiar with the magic powers of midsummer's
night. He ordered the invisible farmer to remove his

shoes. As soon as the farmer had complied with this request, he appeared standing next to his cart in his bare feet. According to the innkeeper a few flowers of the tansy had found their way into his shoes during his nightly journey across the fields. When that happens on midsummer's night between eleven and twelve o'clock it makes the wearer of the shoes invisible.

However, the magic power of the plant will go when the tansy flowers are taken from the shoes.

This is one of the many old legends in which the tansy plays an important role.

In earlier centuries this herb was often picked, dried and used. It was highly valued in a time when dispensing chemists were still to be invented.

The tansy was mainly used to cure intestinal disorders. An extract or tea was made, but it also took the form of various sweets to render the tansy-medicines more tasty. The strongly scented oil is used in some parts of Europe as a pain killer for rheumatism. It is also used for kidney and stomach complaints, but this time as a tansy-bitter made of tansy flowers in brandy.

As this herb is so frequently used, it is hardly surprising to find it in the *Capitulare Villis*, the volume of regulations Charlemagne issued in 812 for the management of his landed and domanial estates. The *Capitulare Villis* contained a list of medicinal herbs, plants and trees that were to be grown in all domains. The tansy was one of them.

In our own environment-conscious time it may be useful to know that tansy keeps flies at a distance with its strongly spicy smell. An extract of tansy may be successfully used against blackfly and greenfly.

The use of the strong firm flowers of the tansy in everlasting bouquets is common knowledge. The plant even owes its name to this fact. Its Latin name, *Tanacetum vulgare*, is derived from the Greek word, 'athanasia' meaning everlasting.

## Biscuits with Tansy

3 eggs
150g (5 oz.) castor sugar
1 packet vanilla sugar
salt
150g (5 oz.) self-raising flour
30g (1½ oz.) cornflour
1 tablespoonful tansy flowers

Pick the flowers of the tansy as soon as the dew has dried.
Discard all green parts and cut up the small yellow
flowers. Beat the eggs with the sugar and vanilla sugar
until frothy. Add the self-raising flour, the salt and the
cornflour. Finally, fold in the pieces of tansy flower.

Do not take more than one tablespoonful of flowers to
three eggs, for these flowers have a strong spicy taste.

Place little heaps of the batter on a buttered baking
sheet, using a tablespoon for measure. During the baking
the biscuits will spread and rise, so leave plenty of
distance between them. Bake the biscuits in a pre-heated
oven at 150°C for twelve to fifteen minutes or until they
are golden brown.

Serve these tansy biscuits regularly to children, since
tansy is one of the best ways of treating, and avoiding
intestinal worms.

## Tansy Cake

1 tablespoonful of tansy flowers
2 tablespoonsful water
100g (4 oz.) margarine or butter
135g (4½ oz.) sugar
2 eggs
75g (3 oz.) plain flour
75g (3 oz.) self-raising flour
75 ml (3 fl.oz.) milk

Cream the butter or margarine with the sugar. Bring the

two tablespoonsful of water to the boil and pour it over the flowers. Leave to soak for five minutes. Strain and add a tablespoonful of this aromatic liquid to the butter. Stir in the eggs one by one and continue to stir until the mixture becomes smooth and light. Stir in the sieved flour, self-raising flour and the milk bit by bit. Fill a buttered cake tin with the batter and bake this lovely scented cake in the oven at 150°C for 1-1½ hours. The cake is done when a knitting needle comes out clean and dry when inserted.

Leave the cake to cook in the tin for a little while, then turn out onto a cake rack.

# Tulips

*Tulipa*

The first tulips appeared in European gardens in the second half of the 16th century. To be more precise, they were first seen in the botanical garden of Augsburg, where it had arrived because of the efforts of Chislaine of Boesbeke, the ambassador of Ferdinand the First in Constantinople.

In Turkey, Chislaine of Boesbeke had been so impressed by the beauty and the splendour of this flower, which had been hitherto unknown to him, that he decided to send a few of its bulbs to Ferdinand the First, who promptly entrusted the botanical garden in Augsburg with them.

The flower was simply named 'tulip', derived from turban, the Turkish headwear.

A few years later the tulip also flowered under the care of the Dutch botanist Christian d' Ecluse in the botanical garden of Leyden. The Tulip soon caught the attention of the Dutch nurserymen. They were totally enthralled and started to devote all their time to experimenting with the tulip. They grew new strains and hitherto unknown shapes and colours. These new tulips were sold at exorbitant prices. The price as well as the rarity made them into status symbols for the rich Dutch merchants of this so-called Golden Age, who outdid one another in pomp and circumstance.

When the prices of tulip-bulbs rose sky-high many saw their chance to make a fortune. The trade that came in existence between 1633 and 1637 is a famous episode in Dutch history. It made many people rich overnight, but equally it ruined many and brought them to acute poverty.

The cultivation and trade of tulips was concentrated round the City of Haarlem and it still is. The bulb fields have grown to be a major tourist attraction in Holland. And small wonder, for fields upon fields of flowering tulips are indeed splendid to behold.

Holland still trades in tulip bulbs and new variations are constantly sought. At this moment over 5,000 species have officially been registered, thanks to the nurserymen who devote all their time to patient and careful cross-breeding, continually even more colourful and spectacular new strains.

During the infamous severe winter of 1944/45, while Holland was still under German occupation, a large part of the tulip bulb stock was eaten by the starving Dutch.

The English, however, have the foremost tulip recipes. The Anglo-Saxons have a centuries-old experience of flower recipes and the tulip forms no exception.

## Tulips with Eggs

**4 large red tulips, without the pistil and stamen**
**4 eggs**
**1 tablespoonful butter**
**1 tablespoonful cream**
**salt and pepper**

Beat the eggs, add the melted butter and the cream and season with the salt and pepper. Fill four small buttered ovenware dishes with the mixture, put them in the oven and allow the egg to set in fifteen minutes at a temperature of approximately 160°C.

When no oven is available this can be done equally well by placing the dishes in a saucepan of boiling water. When the egg mixture has set, the dishes are carefully emptied into the washed and thoroughly dry tulips. Serve as an *entrée*.

## Filled Tulips

**8 beautiful tulips, without pistil and stamen**
**6 large boiled potatoes**
**2 sour apples**
**1 onion**
**1 tablespoonful finely chopped parsley**
**½ teaspoonful finely chopped celery-greens**
**100g (4 oz.) walnuts or mixed nuts**
**4 tablespoonsful oil**
**2 tablespoonsful vinegar**
**salt and pepper**

Cut the peeled and boiled potatoes into small pieces. Peel and core the apples and cut them up too. Chop the onion and the nuts into small bits. Mix all ingredients with the oil and the vinegar. Finally season it with salt and pepper. Leave the salad for at least one hour to allow the tastes to blend.

Finally fill the washed and dried tulips with the potato mixture and serve cold.

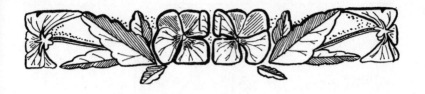

# Violets

*Viola odorata / Viola tricolor*

Viola is a diminutive of the Greek word *vion* indicating fragrant plants. If any plant deserves to be called fragrant, the sweet violet is the one. Its official name is *Viola odorata*. Both names clearly indicate its sweet fragrance, but the English name also indicates its deep blue colour. As this small plant combines such a beautiful fragrance with a modest appearance, the sweet violet is seen as a symbol for humility and fidelity.

Strangely enough this humble little flower became the favourite of one of the most ambitious people in our history, Napoleon Bonaparte.

In order to please her husband, the beautiful Josephine wore a chain of violets in her hair when she was married to Napoleon on 9 March 1796. Napoleon, in gratitude of this thoughtful gesture, would forthwith present her with a posy of freshly picked violets on their wedding anniversary.

This partiality to violets by their General and Emperor-to-be did not remain unnoticed by the French people. They sometimes called him, partly in mockery and partly in admiration, 'Corporal la Violette'.

When Napoleon returned to France from his exile on Elba and started his triumphant march through the

country at the beginning of March 1815, he was welcomed everywhere by ladies dressed in violet gowns, with Sweet Violets in their hair and sprays of sweet violets pinned to their bodices. When he re-entered the Tuileries his admirers had scattered the steps of the palace with sweet violets.

Every self-respecting Roman citizen had at least one bed of scented violets in his garden. To enhance the fragrance even more the Romans planted garlic and onions between the violets, as the Rumanian rose growers even today, plant rows of onions between their rose bushes to make the roses more fragrant.

Pliny advised his fellow Romans to drink violet tea to cure and prevent headaches and hangovers. The *Viola odorata* (i.e. sweet violet) was used for this purpose. Even today it is used for headache and it may also successfully be used to treat disorders of the respiratory tract.

The less fragrant, but certainly equally attractive *Viola tricolor* indicatings its three colours, is mainly used for skin diseases. It is commonly called wild pansy, a name that does this small and pretty flower little justice.

Both types of violets feature strongly in the realm of myths and legends, and there are a great many myths about violets.

One of the most enchanting legends comes from the lands of the Wendish people, a West-Slavonian tribe, living along the banks of the river Elbe. These people managed to maintain many of their old customs until a few years ago. A long, long time ago, the Wendic Kingdom was ruled by a wicked, and evil god named Czorneboh. This evil ruler brought nothing but sorrow and anxiety to the Wendish people. The only good thing about Czorneboh was his lovely daughter.

When the Christian Apostles came to the Wendic Kingdom on their missionary journeys, Czorneboh lost no opportunity to fight these preachers of the new religion. The Christians, however, could count on God's help and they proved to be the stronger in the end. They destroyed the evil power of Czorneboh, who promptly changed into a rock. His lovely daughter changed into a violet that flowers once every one hundred years at the foot of the rock.

The lucky man who picks this violet on Walpurgis Night – the night between 30 April and 1 May – will have the beautiful daughter of Czorneboh for a wife and all his treasures for a dowry.

The legend does not tell if the violet was one of the fragrant purple sweet violets or one of the dainty three-coloured wild pansies, but it is safe to assume that the latter flower is meant as the wild pansy is so much rarer than its purple sister.

The rarity of both flowers has led me to try a few recipes, in which the *Viola odorata* (sweet violet) should have been used, with the *Viola cornuta* (garden pansy) a well-known garden species, which is a purple, fragrant variety.

It appears that this flower can be used as a reasonably good substitute for the sweet violet, which enables us to make a number of recipes without endless searching for the genuine *Viola odorata*.

In salads and soups the three-coloured violets or pansies, that grow in abundance in the wild and can easily be grown in the garden, can freely be used. Do make certain to use the wild variety, though, and not the large overblown flowers without any fragrance at all that can be bought in the shops in Spring.

## Violet Soup

**1 litre (1¾ pt.) of stock**
**40g (1¾ oz.) rice**
**1 teaspoonful lemon juice**
**½ cupful freshly picked violets**

Choose the small purple violets (ideally the sweet violet)

for this recipe. The wild three-coloured violets may be used, but never the large garden-pansies, for they are not fragrant enough.

Boil the rice in the stock for twenty minutes until it is done, add the violets and the lemon juice, simmer gently for another two minutes. Serve immediately.

## Violet Salad

**500g (18 oz.) young endive**
**1 tablespoonful finely chopped celery leaves**
**1 tablespoonful finely chopped parsley**
**1 tablespoonful black olives**
**3 tablespoonsful oil**
**1½ tablespoonsful wine-vinegar**
**salt and sugar to taste**
**30 violets**

Discard any dark green parts of the endive, wash the leaves and allow to drain thoroughly.

Make a dressing of the oil, the vinegar, the salt and the sugar. Cut the endive into very thin strips, add the finely chopped celery and parsley, the olives and the dressing. Toss well. Finally add the petals of the 30 violets and mix the salad gently before serving.

## Violet Rice with mushrooms

200g (7 oz.) Patna-type rice
4½ decilitres (4 fl.oz.) water
salt
250g (9 oz.) edible mushrooms
2 tablespoonsful butter
1 tablespoonful finely chopped parsley
1 tablespoonful violet water
¼ cupful cream
salt
pepper
2 eggs
3 tablespoonsful violet petals

Preferably use the sweet violet for this recipe, though the wild pansy or the purple *Viola cornuta* from the garden may be used as well.

Boil the rice in the ordinary way until it is dry and done. Stew the sliced mushrooms in the butter and add salt and pepper to taste.

Beat the eggs until frothy, add the lukewarm sieved mushrooms, the cream, the violet water and the parsley. Mix well. Fill a buttered ovenproof dish with a layer of cooked rice, a layer of the egg and mushroom mixture, another layer of rice, and so on.

Place the dish in a large saucepan filled with approximately 3 cm (just over 1 inch) of water, and place the pan with the ovenware dish into the oven. Bake the dish at 165°C until golden brown and done.

Sprinkle the finely chopped petals of the violets on the top and serve immediately. A salad tastes good with this dish.

## Deep Fried Violets

Choose sweet violets for this recipe, only if they are absolutely unavailable use the flowers of the purple *Viola cornuta*.

**3 cupsful freshly picked violets**
**3 tablespoonsful cognac or brandy**
**2 tablespoonsful sugar**
**½ teaspoonful cinnamon**
**1 cupful plain flour**
**1 teaspoonful salt**
**3 eggs**
**2 tablespoonsful oil**
**½ cup lager**
**oil to fry**
**a little lukewarm water if required**

Wash the violets and dry them very carefully. Spread the flowers out on a flat surface. Firstly, sprinkle them with the cognac, then with a mixture of sugar and cinnamon.

Whisk the yolks of two of the eggs until they thicken, add the two tablespoons of oil and then slowly one by one a little flour and a little lager until it becomes a smooth batter. A few drops of lukewarm water may be needed if the batter is too stiff.

Beat the three egg whites until they are very stiff, and gently fold them into the batter.

Heat the oil in a fryer, dip the flowers into the batter one by one and quickly fry them golden brown in the hot oil.

Leave them to drain on absorbent kitchen paper and serve them hot, sprinkled with violet sugar. The recipe for violet sugar is given in the chapter on *General ways of preparing flowers* (*Page 11*).

## Violets with Oranges and Lemons

Use the sweet violet or the fragrant purple flowers of the
*Viola cornuta*.

**3 oranges**
**2 lemons**
**3 tablespoonsful butter**
**1 tablespoonful sugar**
**¼ teaspoonful salt**
**1 tablespoonful finely chopped mint leaves**
**3 cupsful violet leaves and flowers**

Peel the oranges and the lemons, remove the pith and
slice them. Remove all pips.

Wash the leaves and flowers of the violets carefully and
dry them thoroughly with paper.

Melt the butter in a frying pan and stew the sliced
oranges and lemons gently for two to three minutes. Add
the leaves and flowers of the violets as well as the salt and
the sugar and continue to simmer for three more
minutes. Serve immediately, garnished with the finely
chopped mint leaves.

## Cake with Violets

**100g (4 oz.) butter or margarine**
**135g (4½ oz.) sugar**
**75g (3 oz.) plain flour**
**75g (3 oz.) self-raising flour**
**2 eggs**
**½ decilitre (2 fl.oz.) milk**
**1 tablespoonful violet water**
**½ cupful icing-sugar**
**crystalized violets for decoration**

The preparation of violet water and crystalized violets
can be found in the chapter on *General ways of preparing
flowers* ( *Page 11*).

Stir the butter and sugar till creamy, add the eggs one

by one and continue to stir until the batter is smooth and light. Mix the plain and the self-raising flour with the milk and the violet water. Gradually add this mixture to the batter, stirring all the time.

Pour the batter into a buttered cake tin, which should be no more than three-quarters full.

Bake the cake in the oven for one to one and a half hours at 150°C. Allow the cake to cool for a few minutes in the tin, before turning it onto a cake rack.

When it has cooled dust the cake generously with the icing-sugar and decorate it with the crystalized violets.

## Sweet Violet dessert

**6 eggs**
**¾ cupful white sugar**
**1 teaspoonful distilled violet water**
**¼ cupful crushed crystalized violets**

Only sweet violets should be used in this recipe because they are the most fragrant.

Beat the yolks of four eggs frothy with the sugar. Add the distilled violet water.

Beat the whites of six eggs very stiff and fold them into the frothy mixture of egg yolk and sugar. Pour this light mixture into a buttered ovenware dish and bake in the oven at 150°C for approximately ten minutes. Sprinkle half the crushed crystalized violets over the dessert, make a cross-like incision in the middle with a fork and put the remainder of the violets into this cut. Bring the temperature of the oven to 165°C and return the dish to the oven for approximately five minutes to become golden brown and fragrant.

Serve hot.

## Violet Soufflé

Choose sweet violets for this recipe. If unavailable the purple *Viola cornuta*.

**25g (1 oz.) butter or margarine**
**25g (1 oz.) plain flour**
**¼ litre (½ pt.) milk**
**2 teaspoonsful distilled violet water**
**2 tablespoonsful sugar**
**½ cupful crystalized violets**
**2 eggs**

Melt the butter, but do not allow it to brown. Add the flour and stirring all the time, the warmed milk and the distilled violet water. Beat the egg yolks and the sugar until they are frothy and add them to the butter and flour mixture. Remove from the heat.

Beat the egg whites very stiff, mix in part of the crystalized violets and fold them gently into the batter, using a metal spoon.

Pour the soufflé batter into a buttered ovenware dish, only half filling it, and place the dish in a preheated oven of 200°C. Bake it in approximately twenty minutes, golden brown. Serve immediately. (Cover the soufflé to avoid deflation) and garnish with the remainder of the crystalized violets at the table.

The recipes for distilled violet water and crystalized violets can be found in the chapter *General ways of preparing flowers* (*Page 11*).

## Violet Jelly

Use sweet violets or purple *Viola cornuta* for this recipe.

**1 cupful of violet petals**
**1½ cupsful water**
**2½ cupsful gelatine**

Wash the flowers, dry them carefully and finely crush them in a liquidizer. Add the water, mix it well and finally stir in the gelatine.

Bring the mixture to the boil and boil briskly for four minutes, unless the instructions on the packet of gelatine say otherwise.

Skim and fill carefully cleaned jam jars with the hot purple jam.

Seal immediately with cellophane paper and store in a cool place.

## Violet Vinegar

**1 cupful violets**
**½ litre (1 pt.) wine-vinegar**

Use only the fragrant sweet violet for this recipe.

Pick the flowers, wash them carefully, dry them and place them in a clean bottle. Add the wine-vinegar, put the bottle in a warm sunny spot and leave it to draw for twenty-four hours.

Filter it through a melitta coffee filter, or a very fine cloth and store this violet vinegar in a cool place. Use in fruit salads.

## Violet Wine à la Appicius

**3 litre (5¼ pt.) red wine**
**3 cupsful freshly picked violets**

Use only the purple sweet violets for this recipe.

Fill a small linen bag with a cupful of freshly picked sweet violet flowers. Hang this bag into the wine and leave it to draw for seven days. Remove the bag and replace it with another bagful of fresh sweet violets. Leave again for seven days. Repeat the procedure once more. Strain the wine and drink it cooled with a little honey.

## Violet Sugar Italian Style

**100g (4 oz.) violets**
**200g (7 oz.) white sugar**

Use sweet violets or purple *Viola cornuta*.

Wash the flower petals and dry them carefully. Pulverise them in a mortar or liquidizer and add the sugar. Spread onto a baking sheet, covered with aluminium foil, and dry carefully in the sun or a luke warm oven. Store this fragrant, colourful sugar in an airtight glass jar.

# Woodruff

*Asperula odorata*

The parents of Mary, mother of Christ, were so poor that they had no money to buy bedding for the cradle of their new-born baby. So Anna went into the fields to look for herbs to line her child's cradle. She noticed the lovely white flowers of Woodruff growing by the side of the road. She picked armsful of this tender plant and filled the cradle with it. At that moment the woodruff started to smell beautifully and it has done so ever since. This scent gave the flower its Latin name *odorata*, while *Asperula* indicated the slight roughness of its leaves. There is every indication that the holy Anna was not the only penniless mother to use woodruff, for many a poor mother did so after her. They, too, knew the sweet scent and gratefully made use of it. The scent of woodruff does not appear to its full advantage until the plant has wilted. Only then is the cumarine released that smells so sweetly.

That is the reason why the English say that woodruff and a rich man's fortune have one thing in common: they can only be enjoyed after death.

In England woodruff is commonly used for its scent. On the 11 June, St Barbara's day, bunches of flowering woodruff are hung in churches and in living rooms.

Woodruff was and still is used to freshen linen in the cupboards. In the north of Holland, young girls used to wear a sprig of woodruff in their bodices. The down-to-earth Northerners gave the plant its nickname, the 'Come-and-Lure-Me-a-Lover' plant.

For internal use, an extract is made of 5g of woodruff flowers and 100 ml (4 fl.oz.) of boiling water. The extract is used to calm the nerves and for insomnia and if we believe the old writings, this draught works better than any one of our modern tranquillizers.

Woodruff is and has long been used in the preparation of May wine, fruit bowl and other sweet delicacies.

## Zabaglione with Woodruff

**5 egg yolks**
**½ litre (1 pt.) wine**
**4 tablespoonsful sugar**
**3 tablespoonsful woodruff flowers**

Mix all the ingredients together in a large fire-proof dish. Place the dish on a pan with boiling water and let the mixture thicken slowly while beating it continuously. When the zabaglione is as thick as custard, it is poured into individual glass dishes and served as a dessert.

## Fruit Bowl with Woodruff

**700g (1½ lb) of strawberries or raspberries**
**200g (7 oz.) castor sugar**
**2 bottles white wine**
**1 lemon**
**a bunch of woodruff**

Carefully wash the berries, remove the green parts, add the sugar and the bunch of woodruff and put in a cool place for at least one hour. Add the juice of the lemon and the wine and leave for at least one more hour. Remove the bunch of woodruff and serve the bowl as cold as possible. It may be garnished with a few woodruff flowers.

## Wine with Woodruff

**1 bottle Moselle wine**
**1 bunch of flowering woodruff**
**50g (2 oz.) sugar**
**1 decilitre (4 fl.oz.) water**
**1 orange**

Pour the wine into a bowl, add the sprigs of woodruff, cover and leave in a cool place for one hour. Strain the wine.

Dissolve the sugar in the water and add the sugar-water to the strained wine.

Squeeze the orange, strain the juice and add it to the wine.

Serve this aromatic drink as cold as possible.

## Fondant with Woodruff

**150g (5 oz.) castor sugar**
**2 to 3 tablespoonsful water**
**2 tablespoonsful woodruff flowers**

Pick the flowers when the dew has dried, wash them carefully, discard all green parts and let them dry on absorbent kitchen paper.

Bring the water and the sugar to the boil and continue to boil until the water has all but evaporated. Test with a spoon. The last drop of sugar-water should form a thin thread. Add the flowers and allow the mixture to cool, by stirring it quickly until it begins to scratch and becomes cloudy. Pour the mixture into buttered shapes or onto a buttered sheet of aluminium foil. As soon as white spots appear on the fondant the shapes are placed upright to cool.

When the fondant has been shaped on the foil, cut it

into squares with a knife dipped in boiling water, as soon
as the mixture has cooled.

## Woodruff Tonic

**1 litre (1¾ pt.) white wine**
**60g (2¼ oz.) woodruff flowers**
**60g (2¼ oz.) sugar**

Pick the flowers when the dew has dried. Mix the washed
and carefully prepared flowers with the sugar. Pour the
wine onto this mixture and leave it in a cool place,
covered with a cloth. The added sugar will ferment the
wine. After two weeks the lightly sparkling wine is
strained and bottled. Cork this wine with care in order to
prevent the corks coming off by themselves. This wine
may be served as an apperitif or may be used as a tonic to
strengthen the heart and kidney functions.